TWO WOMEN
AGAINST THE WIND

A Tierra del Fuego
Bicycling Adventure

Réanne Hemingway-Douglass

Published by Cave Art Press, Anacortes, WA 98221
An imprint of Douglass, Hemingway & Co., LLC
CaveArtPress.com

ISBN-13: 9781934199114

Editor and book designer: Arlene Cook
Additional contributor: Katherine Wells
Manuscript readers: Kathleen Kaska, Rae Kozloff, Lisa Wright
All book photos except where indicated © 2015 Réanne
Hemingway-Douglass
Maps by Ken Morrison

To Katherine, Rina, and all my other wonderful women friends

to Shawn ~

from Léanne Hemingway —
Douglas

CONTENTS

Climbing up Garibaldi Pass

AUTHOR'S NOTE

When my friend Katherine Wells and I set forth to cross Tierra del Fuego on bicycles in 1984, we were both in early middle-age—I was already a grandmother! We undertook this adventure as a personal challenge and it remains, for me, one of the most satisfying experiences of my life. Kathy and I both published articles in bicycling magazines after we returned home to California, but it was always my intention to tell the entire story. For the next three decades, life got in the way, as they say, and I wrote other books. The Tierra del Fuego bicycle trip remained on my list of projects, however, and the time finally arrived when I could sit down and write it.

What follows is an expanded version of the diary I kept for much of the trip. It is an honest account of our adventure, which I hope readers will enjoy for what it is—a three-week snapshot of a raw, remote and extremely beautiful part of the world that few people know much about, even in today's information-driven world. I have returned to Tierra del Fuego several times since our bicycle trip, and the region is more developed than it was in 1984—some stretches of the appalling roads Kathy and I struggled with have been paved, for example. But the scenery and the wildness—not to mention the wind!—remain as they have always been, and I feel privileged to have experienced them.

RHD

Anacortes, Washington, July 2015

Kathy (right) and I, full of energy and optimism in Punta Arenas before setting out on our ride.

PROLOGUE

Wind slammed into us like a truck. It was all Kathy and I could do to hang onto our bikes and keep from being blown over. Riding was impossible, even in the lowest of our eighteen speeds. "Gusts of 70 miles per hour," the ferry boat captain had told us earlier, as we crossed the Straits of Magellan from Punta Arenas, Chile, to begin our cycling trip across Tierra del Fuego. Our arms ached as we shoved the bikes along the gravel road from the ferry landing to the town of Porvenir. With the 40 pounds of gear we each carried in bulky panniers, it was like trying to push an elephant through a wind tunnel.

The gusts intensified, hitting us full in the face. February was supposed to be one of the better summer months for visiting this part of the world, but the wind reminded us that Cape Horn was only 250 miles to the south.

Kathy and I dismounted because we could not control our bikes. In the strongest gusts we had to stop, lay the bikes on the ground, and wait until we could push forward again. Porvenir, our first stop, was a mere three miles from the ferry landing. Ushuaia, our ultimate goal, was nearly 300 miles away. Would the wind be like this all the way?

Dust and sand blasted our faces. I was chewing grit. Kathy looked at me through her goggles and shouted something that I could barely hear, but that would become a recurring refrain in the days ahead: "Who the hell had this idea anyway?"

Map 1: Southern Chile & Argentina
Showing Location of Tierra del Fuego

CHAPTER 1

PUNTA ARENAS

Friday, January 27, 1984: Tightening my seatbelt, I settled back in the seat of the Boeing 727 and glanced at my watch. Two hours till we landed in Punta Arenas, the southernmost city in Chile. I was nervous and excited, as was my friend, Katherine Wells. I had been planning this trip for months, but Kathy had decided to join me only a few weeks previously. For me, it was a sentimental homecoming of sorts, and for both of us it would be a major test of our physical and mental capabilities. Our luggage included two dismantled mountain bikes. When we arrived in Punta Arenas, Kathy and I would reassemble them, cross the Strait of Magellan, and begin a mountain biking trip that would push our middle-aged female bodies to the ultimate—a nearly 300-mile trip across Tierra del Fuego, the "uttermost part of the earth."[1]

Kathy and I had boarded the flight to Punta Arenas in Santiago, the Chilean capital, after leaving Los Angeles the previous day. Our airborne route south followed the edge of the Andes, allowing those of us in window seats glimpses of thickly forested uninhabited valleys cut by rivers that ran to the Pacific; volcano after volcano with battle-scarred craters; snow fields and glaciers. Then the pilot announced that we were over Puerto Montt, the last city on the Chilean coast before the Patagonian waterways and archipelagos begin. Memories flooded my mind as I looked down on Golfo de Penas, the northernmost entry to the Canales de Patagonia. My husband,

1

Don, and I had sailed these waterways nine years earlier in our damaged sailboat, under the most extreme conditions possible. My throat tightened as I studied the channels and fjords below. Don would love this, I thought. He'd be thrilled to see this region from an airplane. His nose, like mine, would be glued to the window, and he'd be giving a running account of what he recognized. Don, in fact, had wanted very much to come with us, but I had uninvited him. I had spent all seventeen years of my marriage to Don going along with him, at his driven pace, on his terms—and always lagging behind. So often he made me feel inadequate. But now I had a goal of my own to fulfill, and I was determined to do it my way. My longtime friend Kathy was a woman whose fitness level and determination were comparable to my own. She and I would ride across Tierra del Fuego together.

As Punta Arenas neared, I wondered what changes I might find. In 1975, Don and I had spent three months there, after being pitchpoled (i.e., flipped 360°) in our sailboat by a rogue wave halfway between Easter Island and Cape Horn. After recovering our energies, we considered what to do next. Punta Arenas was the largest city on any continent south of the 46th parallel, and the capital of the Chilean province of Magallanes. In 1975, it had a population of 80,000 or so, yet Don and I had found it difficult to communicate with the outside world.[2] The telephone system at that time was so antiquated we used a friend's ham radio to patch through to our families back in the States. The port facilities had been a challenge for us too. Punta Arenas was an open roadstead, meaning it did not have a harbor, merely a long pier owned by the Chilean Navy that jutted 400 yards out into the Strait of Magellan. Tied up along the pier, or rafted to other vessels, our 42-foot sailboat, *Le Dauphin Amical*, was mercilessly exposed to the wind and waves. Don and I could never leave her for more than a few hours at a time in case the wind changed direction, requiring us to move from one side of the pier to the other. In letters home, I wrote that playing "ring around the pier" was an all-consuming pastime.

Perhaps a new port had been built in the nine years since then? I wondered, too, if the port's boat repair facilities had been expanded. *Le Dauphin* had been seriously damaged by the pitchpole. When we finally limped into Punta Arenas 42 days later, we were able to replace some broken spars and other small fittings. However, no facilities existed at that time for hauling out a boat of *Le Dauphin's* size to make major repairs, and we were forced to head to Buenos Aires—a thousand miles to the north.

The pilot's voice jogged me back to the present: "If you look out the right side of the plane, you can see Canal Trinidad and Isla Madre de Dios." I scrambled over and looked down on a jigsaw puzzle—green and dazzling white, surrounded by blue waters. It's so beautiful, I thought! Don and I had first entered the Patagonian waterways through Canal Trinidad. And somewhere down there was Dársena Aid (Aid Basin), where violent, unpredictable "williwaw" gusts had slammed us every night at anchor.

The plane was beginning its descent across the silver radiance of Canal Sarmiento and Seno Union (Union Sound). Punta Arenas was a mere forty-five minutes away. Circular rainbows appeared through the clouds as we caught a glimpse of the cathedral-like peaks rising out of beautiful Torres del Paine National Park. Chills ran through me. We were nearly there. I was almost as excited as I had been when Don and I pulled up to the Punta Arenas pier in April 1975. I felt like I was coming home, and the big test was about to begin.

The plane landed in early evening and an airport bus delivered Kathy, me and our bikes to the door of our hotel, the Savoy. Though not as luxurious as its name suggested, the Savoy was clean, with private bathrooms. The hospitable staff went out of their way to welcome us and all our gear. In fact, they became our psychological support staff as Kathy and I assembled our bikes and panniers the following morning. We tried to imagine the personnel at an American hotel greeting us in the same way, but the only visions we could conjure up were of pursed lips and disdainful looks.

In this respect, Punta Arenas was as I remembered it. Don and I had been the recipients of generous and gracious hospitality during our 1975 visit. On the day we arrived in our battered boat (April 14, 1975), a crowd of people stood on the pier to welcome us. Even before we'd completed arrival formalities, Erwin Korn, the director of the local yacht club, offered the use of his washing machine. Humberto Gaete from the amateur Radio Club asked if we'd like to contact our family in the States. His wife, Pepita, an English teacher, wanted to show us around town immediately. We made many friends over the next couple of months, as people continually came down to the pier, introduced themselves, and invited us to join them for tea, for a ride, or for dinner. A language teacher myself, I gravitated particularly towards the educators in Punta Arenas and was invited to talk at a number of local schools. Don complained that our social life was so full we barely had time to do any work on the boat—though he enjoyed socializing as much as I did.

We were grateful also for the courtesy and helpfulness shown to us by the Chilean Navy, whose official guests we were for the duration of our stay. Chile, at that time, and in 1984 also, was subject to the dictatorship of General Augusto Pinochet. Punta Arenas, like everywhere, was under military occupation—but the officers with whom Don and I came into contact were unfailingly polite and patient with us.

Don and I had also enjoyed the cosmopolitan flavor of Punta Arenas. The city had been founded in 1848 as a penal colony by the Chilean Government as a means of asserting sovereignty over the Strait of Magellan and as a disciplinary post for military personnel with problematic behavior.

However, free settlers of various nationalities found their own ways to Punta Arenas in the decades that followed, attracted by a gold rush and a sheep farming boom in the late nineteenth century. Don and I found modern-day Punta Arenas to be a surprising melting pot of nationalities, with many people of British, German, Croatian and French descent. Though some were of the second and third generations, many were intent on keeping their mother language and so were bilingual, with each culture retaining traditions of its own. Thus, among our friends, the English Campbell family sent its children to the British school and observed "elevenses"—British tea-time, so named because it was originally served at 11 a.m. The Korn family sent their children to the German school. The Alliance Française provided French lessons and social gatherings for French descendants and Francophiles alike. A visit to the cemetery attested further to the diversity of the population.

Architecturally, the city had a run-down colonial appearance in 1975, but by 1984 oil money and government subsidies had enhanced its face. New housing units, renovations to old buildings, along with satellite telecommunications, and same-day air shipments of produce and groceries, had linked the city to the rest of Chile. It seemed to me that fewer soldiers inhabited the street corners, and the *carabineri* (soldiers) now carried sticks, rather than guns.

Only the weather remained unchanged—and, indeed, one of the reasons I wanted to return to Punta Arenas was to confirm that the weather was truly as wild as I remembered it. Don and I had been there from April to early June, the austral autumn, and the wind had blown relentlessly, at gale strength or more, almost every day. The only variation was in the direction, which changed from one day to the next, and often several times in one day. As the season progressed we experienced snowstorms as well, and on fine mornings we would wake to find our decks and rigging coated with ice.

Kathy and I arrived at the height of the austral summer. Freezing conditions in Punta Arenas or Tierra del Fuego were unlikely, and it would never be too hot to ride bicycles, but the wind and unpredictable weather changes would be a constant reality. Tierra del Fuegian naturalist and author Natalie Goodall (whom Kathy and I were to visit on our trip) advised in her 1979 artistic guidebook to the region that "the best months to visit...are from November until the end of April." She noted that summer was one of the windiest seasons, however, and "no one can count on the weather... Rain showers may be interspersed with bright sun bursts throughout the day."[3]

Yes, the weather would be a challenge—but for me it was also one of the attractions of this raw land, and a nemesis to conquer. Had I wanted an easy ride beneath blue skies and sunshine, I would have stayed home in California.

Saturday, January 28: On our first full day in Punta Arenas, Kathy and I arose early and spent the morning doing errands, including making arrangements for further travel in Chile after our bicycle trip. I did not know the woman in the travel agency, but when I mentioned having been in Punta Arenas with Don eight years earlier, she remembered the newspaper and television coverage of our visit. Only a few sailboats a year ever called in Punta Arenas then, and after our pitchpoling ordeal Don and I had been feted as minor celebrities.

In the early afternoon, my friend Rina, a French teacher whose classroom I had visited in 1975, picked up Kathy and me from the Savoy and took us home for a delicious lunch: scallops, avocados, and tomatoes for appetizers; chicken and soufflé potato balls for main course; and a light cherry-flavored *crema* for dessert. Since Kathy and I both spoke Spanish, we conversed in that language with Rina and her family over lunch. Kathy and I talked about our hopes for our bike trip. Rina and her husband, Sergio, a lawyer, warned us about Tierra del Fuego road conditions, but also offered information about routes, *estancias* (ranches), climate and so forth. They would be visiting the region themselves in just a couple of days and, with luck, we would see them on the road.

One thing I hadn't managed to do on my first visit to Punta Arenas with Don was to visit the *Penguinéria*—the local penguin rookery. When I asked Sergio about it, he said, *"Muchos penguinos en sus nidos.* (Many penguins in their nests.) Let's go!" The rookery was further away than I had expected, across gravel and dirt roads with no signposts along the way. Had Kathy and I attempted to find our own way there, we would have been lost for sure. As far as I could figure out, the rookery was on Seno Otway (Otway Sound), 20 miles or so northwest of Punta Arenas. Waves battered the shore as we arrived, and a cold wind was blowing, but the weather improved as the afternoon progressed.

The penguins, of which there were indeed many, were of the Magellanic variety (*Spheniscus magellanicus*). They were a bit over two feet tall, with black backs, white fronts, and black bands across their faces and necks. Found only in South America and the Falkland Islands, they gather in large colonies on shore, where they lay one or two eggs a year in burrow-like nests. Mating pairs remain bonded to one another for life, and they return to the same nest every year.

Kathy collected penguin bones for her teenage son and we took photos of penguins and their nests. The ground cover at the rookery resembled miniature ferns, hard to the touch but with moss-like contours and succulent roots. There were also ground-hugging shrubs, similar to the alpine tundra species found in the North Cascades of Washington State, where Don and I now live.

Above: Magellanic penguins, Seno Otway.

Below: At home with Rina, her husband Sergio, and their son Mauricio.

We returned to Rina and Sergio's for tea. Having caught up on family matters over lunch, the conversation turned to more general topics. While Punta Arenas looked more prosperous than it had eight years earlier, Rina said that construction projects had slowed of late due to the state of the Chilean economy. She also said that education had gone downhill and teachers were accorded less respect. However, Punta Arenas—and Magallanes province—had fewer drug problems than *al norte*.

Most people, Rina and Sergio included, had little idea of what was going on in the rest of the world, as limited international news was published in Chile. Sergio said that Chile was the only country which had been able to throw off its Communist shackles. I remarked that there seemed to be fewer guns in sight than in 1975, but Sergio told us the *carabineri* still conducted routine identification checks on citizens and tourists.

We talked about Argentina also, since the eastern half of Tierra del Fuego is Argentine. Don and I had found Chile to be a much more agreeable country than Argentina, and I imagined little had changed in the interim. Sergio said Argentines were lazy. "They go to the beach and drink *mate* [a highly caffeinated tea-like beverage]. They'll have to learn to work if they want to improve their economy. They have the capacity to nourish all of South America, but they don't."

Rina drove us back to the Savoy after tea so Kathy and I could finish our packing. She offered to store any items we didn't want to take with us on the bike trip, and she returned later in the evening with her twenty-four-year-old son, Mauricio, in their four wheel-drive Toyota to pick up our extra belongings.

Sunday, January 29, a.m.: Because Punta Arenas sits at the bottom of mainland South America, Kathy and I would have to take a *barcaza* (car ferry) across the Strait of Magellan to get to the main island of Tierra del Fuego. We rose at 6:30 a.m. to have "plenty of time" before the 9 a.m. sailing. At first we had trouble mounting our bags on the bikes, then realized that the baggage racks themselves were incorrectly mounted. With no time to fix the problem, we forced the bags onto the bikes and departed the Savoy. When we arrived at the ferry dock, we found we had mistaken the sailing time and were an hour early.

The *barcaza*, the *Melinka,* was a red-painted landing transport craft with an open car deck at the bow and a cabin and engine room at the stern. I read on a plaque that she had been built in Dade County, Florida, and realized she was the same vessel on which Don and I had made several crossings of the Strait nine years before.

Kathy and I wheeled our bikes aboard and I asked if we could go into the cabin. No, not before 4 p.m.: "*La barcaza tiene problemas con el motor.* (The ferry has engine problems.)" I went up to the wheelhouse to meet the captain and explained who I was. He turned out to be Captain Raúl, the former skipper of the *Calabria,* a fishing vessel Don and I had come to know well in 1975, since *Le Dauphin* had frequently rafted up against *Calabria* at the Punta Arenas pier. Don and I had been looking for additional crew for our onward journey to Buenos Aires, and Captain Raúl had recommended one of his own crewmen, Alfonso Bahamonde, as a young man who would benefit from the experience. Alfonso subsequently joined us aboard *Le Dauphin* and remained part of the crew for the next year.[4] Now he lived on the southern Chilean island of Chiloé. I told Raúl that Kathy and I planned to visit Alfonso before we flew back to California.

With half a day to kill, Kathy and I returned to the Savoy and figured out the correct way to mount the baggage racks. The panniers now mounted much more easily. The bags were Kangaroo Baggs, produced by the company Don and I had started in 1970 to manufacture backpacks. In the 1980s we expanded into mountain biking accessories and clothing, and as CEO of the corporation, Don expected all bicycling events in which we took part to generate publicity for the company. Our current expedition was no different. It also presented an opportunity to test our gear under the most challenging conditions possible. Kathy and I had yet to set foot on Tierra del Fuego and already my diary included the notes: *Mountain Bagg Stuff Sack—poor placement of compression straps. Straps for securing panniers too long or Velcro in wrong place.*

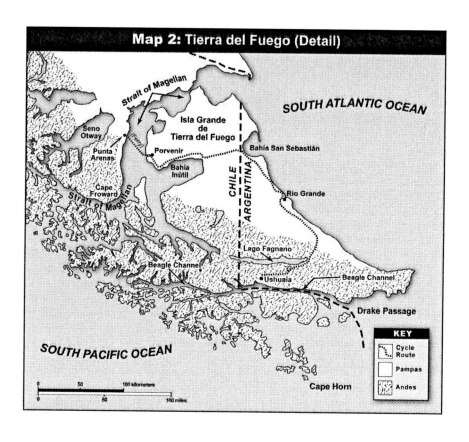

Map 2: Tierra del Fuego (Detail)

Strait of Magellan

SOUTH ATLANTIC OCEAN

Seno Otway

Isla Grande de Tierra del Fuego

Punta Arenas

Porvenir

Bahía San Sebastián

Bahía Inútil

CHILE

ARGENTINA

Cape Froward

Strait of Magellan

Rio Grande

Lago Fagnano

Beagle Channel

Ushuaia

Beagle Channel

Drake Passage

SOUTH PACIFIC OCEAN

0   50   100 kilometers
0   50   100 miles

Cape Horn

KEY

Cycle Route

Pampas

Andes

12

CHAPTER 2

PUSHING TO USHUAIA

The route Kathy and I planned to ride was a traverse of Isla Grande of Tierra del Fuego. This "big island" is what most people think of as "Tierra del Fuego," though Tierra del Fuego actually comprises a vast archipelago of thousands of islands. Only a handful of these are inhabited; many remain unexplored, and some are little more than rocks. Geographically, Tierra del Fuego is situated just below the bottom tip of continental South America. It is bounded by the Strait of Magellan to the north, and by the Atlantic, Pacific and Southern Oceans to the east, west and south, respectively. Its southernmost extremity is Cape Horn, which is itself an island. Geologically, Tierra del Fuego is a continuation of both the South American Pampa and the Andes. It is a region of spectacular scenery—a frontier land of fjords, glaciers, streams and waterfalls, dense beech forests and wind-sculpted cypress trees, as well as brown rolling hills, mudflats— and sheep. It is infamous for wild weather, though British explorers of the nineteenth century found the climate of Isla Grande "not unlike that of northern England."[5]

These days, Tierra del Fuego is a stopping-off place for well-to-do tourists who depart from the southern port of Ushuaia on cruise ships to Antarctica. However, for the longest time Isla Grande existed mostly in people's imaginations—as a land of romance and mystery, conjuring up images of shipwrecks, Indians, missionaries, and adventurers, including the

English writer Bruce Chatwin, who turned a 1975 visit to southern Argentina and Tierra del Fuego into a best-selling travel memoir, *In Patagonia.*[6] For literary purposes Chatwin considered Tierra del Fuego to be part of Patagonia, but locals prefer to be called Fuegians, rather than Patagonians. Natalie Goodall, a naturalized Fuegian, says, "it is felt that Patagonia ends at the Strait of Magellan."[7]

In English, the name Tierra del Fuego means "Land of Fire." The first European to lay eyes on it was Ferdinand Magellan, who visited in 1520 during his historic first circumnavigation of the globe. He supposedly named the region *Tierra del Humo* (Land of Smoke) after sighting Indian fires along its shores. But according to history, his patron, King Charles V of Spain, argued there was no smoke without fire, and rechristened the new land *Tierra del Fuego*. (While there are still fires to be seen in the north of Isla Grande, these are mostly flares from oil and gas wells.)

The most famous visitor to the region after Magellan was probably Charles Darwin. He was serving as naturalist aboard HMS *Beagle* when the ship sailed around the bottom of South America on her own famous circumnavigation of 1831-36. The *Beagle* had visited Tierra del Fuego on a previous voyage in 1830, and her captain, Robert FitzRoy, had kidnapped four Fuegian (Yahgan) natives and taken them back to London, where he educated them at his own expense and presented them to the Royal Court. On the *Beagle's* second voyage to the region, with Darwin aboard, the three surviving Yahgans—Jemmy Button, Fuegia Basket and York Minster— were returned to their homeland, dressed in European clothes and with such "civilized" accoutrements as chamber pots, table linen and wine glasses. FitzRoy's hope was that the three would spread the word of God to their fellow natives.

At that time, four distinct tribes of Indians inhabited Tierra del Fuego; of these, the Yahgans and Alacaluf were "canoe people," who lived along the shorelines; the Ona and Haush were nomadic hunters who roamed the interior of Isla Grande. Physically and culturally, all were well adapted to the region, yet they were deemed by Europeans to be among the most depraved people on earth, by reason of their geographical remoteness from Europe and the Holy Lands. Darwin thought the Fuegians in their natural habitat were closer to wild animals than human beings—a notion that remained with him when he eventually came to write *The Descent of Man*. Darwin was less surprised than FitzRoy when the three Yahgans rapidly reverted to their traditional ways after being set ashore on Navarin Island, south of the Beagle Channel.[8]

Tierra del Fuego's first permanent European settlers were missionaries who arrived in 1871. They were followed by sheep farmers, gold miners, and merchants of various nationalities, all of whom lived in "extremely primitive conditions."[9] The missionaries gradually gained the trust of the natives, but the Fuegian Indians eventually died out, victims of European diseases and/or of white ranchers who killed them for poaching sheep. No pure-blood Fuegian natives survived beyond 1920, although a number of their mixed-race descendants survive on Isla Grande.

Politically, Tierra del Fuego has been divided since 1881 between Chile and Argentina. On Isla Grande, the international border runs more or less down the middle of the island, north-south along latitude 68°36'W. Chile controls the western half, Argentina the eastern. The combined region is, as Goodall notes, "slightly larger than the island of Ceylon, somewhat smaller than Ireland."[10] It is sparsely populated, with just three significant towns—Porvenir, Río Grande and Ushuaia—all on Isla Grande. There are also a number of smaller settlements. At the time of our bike trip, Porvenir, on the Chilean side of Isla Grande, had a population of about 4,000; Río Grande and Ushuaia, on the Argentine side, were larger, with approximately 9,000 and 7,000 residents, respectively. All were modern towns in 1984, with Río Grande the focus of considerable industrial development, but the main road that links all three towns was unpaved for almost its entire length—which added considerably to the challenge of our bicycle venture.

The southern half of Isla Grande comprises mountains and swamps. The rest of the landscape is divided into large, self-sufficient sheep ranches, called *estancias*. (The Spanish word *estancia* may also refer to the location of the ranch buildings, or homestead, on each property.) Natalie Goodall noted in her 1979 guidebook that there were about 60 *estancias* in Argentine Tierra del Fuego at that time, running a total of 780,000 sheep and 15,000 cattle. These were modern commercial operations and were invariably large because the quality of land is such that it takes about three acres to support a single sheep. The *estancias* were traditionally hospitable to travelers, but had become less so with the rise in tourism in the region. Kathy and I were cautioned that we should not look to *estancias* as places to stay, and that we should visit them only if we were invited to do so. (There were hotels in the towns, however, and a number of *hosterías*, small hotels or hostels, in various places along the way.)

Sunday, January 29, 4 p.m.: The *Melinka* finally departed for its three hour crossing to Tierra del Fuego, with Kathy and me and our repacked bicycles aboard. The wind and seas worsened as we proceeded across the Strait. The vessel shuddered and cracked down into 10- to 15-foot waves. One wave broke over the bow, soaking the autos, trucks and bikes. Standing beside Captain Raúl in the wheelhouse, I could see the concern on his face. The whole Strait was a mass of white that reminded me of the crossings Don and I had made on the *Melinka* in 1975, when we spent three weeks in the relatively sheltered haven of Bahía Chilota, on the Tierra del Fuego side of the Strait. Although the winds howl just as strongly in

Boarding the Melinka.

Captain Raúl watching the weather.

Bahía Chilota, there are no swells. Fishermen from Punta Arenas take their boats there to do maintenance work, and Don and I had done the same with *Le Dauphin*. Bahía Chilota has a narrow, serpentine entrance, challenging to negotiate even for skilled boatmen. Captain Raúl reminded me that Don and I had taken a sailor from Punta Arenas to help us navigate the channel safely. But Raúl and his crew managed it successfully now, and a short time later we pulled into the small dock at Chilota. Raúl said, *"De vuelta escribire a Alfonso."* ("I will write a letter to Alfonso for you to deliver after your return journey.") *"Ahora tengo que. . .* (And now...)", he added, pointing to his eye, meaning it was time to turn his attention to docking.

As Kathy and I disembarked, 35- to 45-mile-an-hour winds met us in the face. This was merely the base strength. Raúl had warned us to expect gusts of 70 miles per hour. Our bags were soaked, the Spenco seat covers were heavy with absorbed water. Same story with the inside of my bicycle helmet. Kathy looked at me and shouted through one of the gusts, "Who the hell had this idea anyway?!"

By this time it was early evening. The landscape around Bahía Chilota was dry and flat compared to the Punta Arenas side of the Strait, which was more pastoral with a backdrop of mountains. Don and I had found a stark beauty in what we had seen of Tierra del Fuego, but on this day I was in no mood for aesthetic appreciation. The small town of Porvenir was three miles down the road and we needed to get there before dark. We had camping gear in our panniers but we hoped to find the Porvenir equivalent of the Savoy.

We started out determined to buck the wind, but after a couple of revolutions of the pedals we realized it was impossible to control our bikes, even in the lowest gear. Riding was just too dangerous on the gravel road. Cars came by at 40 miles an hour or more without moving over, kicking up gravel and dust all over us. We dismounted and pushed our bikes to the edge of Porvenir. The gusts grew stronger, some reaching what I estimated to be Captain Raúl's forecast 70 miles per hour. We had to stop, lay our bikes on the ground, and wait for the gusts to pass. Even then, the wind was so strong we could barely walk. It was like trying to maneuver the helm of *Le Dauphin* in a gale. Without the heavy bags on our front wheels, our bikes would have been carried away. We needed our goggles. Dust and sand blew into our eyes, up our noses, and into our mouths. I was chewing grit.

Kathy's recollection: *We were forced to get off the bikes. There was no way we could control them. We lay down in the sandy soil beside the road and braced ourselves against the wind's assault. Blast after blast scoured our faces and any other accessible body part. "Jesus," I thought. "How are we ever going to be able to ride anywhere in wind like this?" I realized how stupid I was. I could never have imagined trying to ride under such God-awful conditions.*

Hunkering there, trying to be stoic when I was scared to death, I wondered what we would do, how long the wind would lash at us. Would we have to spend the night here? We might as well have been pinned down by gunfire...

But we struggled on, pushing our bikes until we finally arrived at the edge of Porvenir—a street where a bronze statue with a white wall around it offered shelter from the wind. Kathy and I decided we'd have to try to make it all the way into the town. Just then a teenage-boy appeared, materializing as if from nowhere. To him, we must have looked like two half-dead creatures washed up on a beach. To us, he was the angel of mercy.

"*Puerdo ayudarlas?* (Can I help you?)" he asked.

Kathy asked if he knew where we could find a hotel. He pointed down the hill. "Would you like me to see if they have a room?"

"Please!"

The boy was back in two minutes, said we could stay there, and he'd show us the way. He helped us lift our bikes upright again and accompanied us as we pushed into further volleys of wind towards the hotel, the Hostería Flamencos. We had to lift the bikes over a log fence to get to there. The front entrance was on the far side of the building, but the woman at the desk didn't seem happy about letting us enter that way with our bikes and directed us through the back entrance. The boy said goodbye and ran on home without expecting anything from us. I remarked to Kathy that if we were in Mexico, rather than Chile, he'd have stood there until we paid him. The hotel had a restaurant, so we ate dinner there. Kathy asked the waitress if she knew the boy, because we wanted to give him a small gift. The waitress replied that she did, and that she would deliver it to him.

As we waited for our meal, Kathy and I speculated about what might have happened if the *barcaza* had not been delayed. We might be out in the wind, on the far side of Porvenir, trying to camp somewhere. We discussed what we'd do if we were forced to camp in similar conditions. I was not sure the tent would hold up in such a gale. Perhaps we could use the bikes to anchor the tent in some way?

Back in our room, we hung our clothes and bags on the furniture to dry. This messed up the decor, but it was better than spending the night in the tent.

Kathy said, "Don says we must have a goal every day. I think our goal for today was Porvenir."

Porvenir or bust! If we had gone beyond it today we *would* have bust.

So, who the hell *did* have the idea for this crazy trip? I did. My goal was to ride all the way across Tierra del Fuego, from Porvenir at the top, to Ushuaia at the bottom—a 300-mile bicycle trip on dirt and gravel roads, that would begin by following the Strait of Magellan, turn east across the middle of the island to the Atlantic, then head southwest. There would be several passes to climb at the bottom end of the Andes, but most of the route would be across pampa and rolling hills. To the uninitiated it might sound easy, but I knew there would be the wind to contend with. Always the wind. . .

Kathy was my accomplice. I had asked her a year earlier, when I was formulating the trip in my mind, if she would come with me. She had said no, and another woman friend, Ann, agreed to accompany me. But six weeks before we were due to leave, Ann discovered she was pregnant.

As Kathy tells it, I phoned her "almost before Ann's lab report hit the gynecologist's desk."[11]

21

"Come on, Kath," I urged her. "You can get in shape." Kathy recalls that my voice was "determinedly bright." She didn't know if I thought she really could do it, or if I was simply afraid to go alone. My answer to that was—both.

A writer and artist by profession, Kathy was between projects—she could arrange the time. She would talk to a physical trainer, she said, and ask his opinion about the wisdom of taking a 300-mile bicycle trip at the bottom of the earth, leaving in four to five weeks.

She was 47, and had never ridden more than a few miles in one stretch, even as a child. As an adult she had done a lot of backpacking and sailing, but nothing strenuous like tennis or aerobics classes. She was asthmatic and could only do activities where she controlled the pace. In recent years she had done little more than pound typewriter keys. The trainer she consulted ("an immaculate specimen, thirty years younger than me, straight out of a shampoo commercial") asked her if she planned to "pedal with her fingers." He declared she'd be lucky if she came out of it without a serious injury. At best it would be no fun, like trying to run the Boston Marathon cold.

Kathy being Kathy, she sought a second opinion from someone more likely to talk her into it—a friend who poo-poohed the trainer: "Does he know what a hard-ass you are?" The friend, a fanatic cyclist and ex-swimming coach, knew what the trainer didn't—that Kathy usually did whatever she was determined to do, that her mind would be at least fifty percent of the equation. I knew that about her too, which was why I had pegged her from the outset as the obvious person to go with me. She was also drawn to the unusual—the odd, wild places where "man's inroads remain unpaved. . . Perhaps it's a pilgrimage syndrome, or a dark cast of mind—a capacity for intense pleasure, but little interest in 'fun.'"

I was a couple of years older than Kathy (I would celebrate my 51st birthday in Tierra del Fuego), but I had already been training seriously for several months on Don's custom-built Ritchie mountain bike. Don and I lived in the Sierras at that time, and I rode 20-25 miles a day at 7,000-foot elevations. I also had Don, a super-athlete himself, as my coach. Kathy's friend knew from cycling that the body can condition itself rapidly if the process is done right. Kathy herself was still equivocating ("Why not just spend my travel budget on a Club Med vacation, or go visit a friend in Hawaii who had been nagging me to come?") when she sought a third opinion from a doctor who was also a serious cyclist. "No problem," he said. He was 62 but often did 75-mile rides on his Saturdays. "Let your body be your guide," he told her, adding that he expected to see her photos when she returned.

The clincher was a recent dream she'd had about a bicycle that had stuck in her mind like a feathered hook—"a telegram from her psyche," as she called it. She admitted that for months she'd felt vague stirrings about doing something intensely physical. She was also going through shifts in major areas of her life. The trip could be an opportunity to step back and reassess, get new bearings. "Like binoculars, desire and opportunity were coming into focus."

Don had phoned Kathy to provide encouragement and training suggestions: "Begin slowly. Give your body a warning." She jumped rope, did stretches, rode her rusty old 10-speed around the neighborhood, riding a little further each time. She installed some bike rollers in her garage so she could train at night. She found the "garage rides" both grueling and tedious, though she reported that her 12-year-old son began to regard her "with an altered light in his eyes—something between incredulity and respect." My own reaction was the same: one Sunday, a couple of weeks into her training, I met up with her and together we cycled thirty miles in three hours. "A month ago that would have seemed like going to China," she told me. She was also enjoying the fact that with all this exercise she no longer needed to count calories and could "eat with impunity—lasagna, French toast, guacamole, all with absolute lust!"

Finally, she took the leap and bought an all-terrain Fisher bike and all the accoutrements. We both understood that with this purchase she was truly committed—she had spent too much to turn back. She drove with her new bike to our house in the Eastern Sierra to finalize our plans and test our clothing and equipment. The two of us needed to work out signals and practice drafting (an energy-saving technique that proved to have no relevance in Tierra del Fuego). We rode from the valley in Bishop up the Old Sherwin summit, climbing 3,000 feet in four miles and ending in snow at 7,000 feet. Kathy celebrated the fact that she had kept up with me—an irony, in retrospect, given that I would ultimately spend much of our Tierra del Fuego ride trying to keep up with her.

Four weeks into her training, Kathy joined Don and me in a 100-mile Race Across America qualifying ride. The svelte racing machines of the superstar cyclists leaped out of sight, as Don did too, before Kathy and I had even crossed the start line on our stolid fat-tired bikes. I was recovering from a cold. Neither of us had ridden 100 miles before. We decided just to do what we could do. We weren't racing, after all, just extending our limits. The weather turned surly and our hands and feet grew numb, as we were inadequately dressed. When we stopped for lunch at the 35-mile post, the lead racers passed us on their return trip. Kathy and I finished eating and headed back, completing 70 miles by the time we reached the parking lot. We were tired but confident. We both understood that Tierra del Fuego would be our own private contest, with a moveable finish line. If we managed to ride 70 miles in a day on our trip, great, but Kathy and I were the only two people to whom it would matter.

Kathy, in training in California.

Monday, January 30: Our windows rattled until midnight, when the wind finally let up. I fell asleep feeling more hopeful. But by morning the wind had picked up again and, from the window of the Hostería Flamencos, we could see white caps on Bahía Chilota.

After a fruitless attempt to locate a family Don and I had befriended in 1975, Kathy and I set forth from Porvenir at 11:30 a.m. The wind was blowing 40 miles per hour and gusting a little higher. We were able to remain on our bikes in town, where the houses gave us some protection, but once we got out onto the road it was a different story. Earlier that morning, we had asked a woman at the *museo* about routes out of town. One new road went east, she told us. The other—which I knew from the map—went south. We set off along the new road. When we had pedaled a quarter-mile or so, eight little kids yelled at us that it was *"muy duro"* ("very difficult"), so we re-traced our route to a fork in the road, asked again for directions, and headed south.

Beyond Porvenir, a gravel road stretched before us. The wind was in our faces and too fierce for riding, just as it had been the evening before. We had no choice but to walk, pushing our bikes. "This is the pits," I thought, "I've come ten thousand miles to push a bicycle?" I composed a telex in my mind to send to Don: "Pushing to Ushuaia. Knuckles white. Face sandblasted." I remembered his coaching: "Draft. Stay on each other's tails." Draft? Hell! We were doing that, but walking, not riding. I was in the lead and had to hunch my neck to minimize my exposure to the blowing sand and gravel.

Kathy told me later that if she'd had the energy to spare in the wind, she said, she would have screamed at me: "What the hell made you think we could do this?" As we forged on, I pondered the reasons that had compelled me, a middle-aged grandmother, to subject myself to this ordeal. I had turned fifty the previous year and wanted to test myself—not against

Don, at *his* competitive pace, on *his* terms, but with another woman like myself. I wanted to do something epic and physical that would be within my capabilities—not something that had the potential to kill me (as my 1975 sailing voyage with Don had nearly done). I had a compulsion to return to this harsh, dramatically beautiful land, where Don and I had lived for three months under conditions of great physical duress while enjoying fantastic hospitality. What better way to get reacquainted with the land and its people than on a bicycle? Ego had played a part in my thinking as well: "Kathy and I could be the first 'women's cycling team' to cross Tierra del Fuego!"

But now I was sure I'd made a mistake. Good Lord, I couldn't ride in these conditions for nearly 300 miles. I felt guilty, wondering if I'd downplayed the severity of the weather to Kathy when she first expressed interest in coming with me. Had I even downplayed it to myself? "Damn it," I told myself, "I can't worry about how Kathy feels. She's here because she wants to be. We're going to make it. Just shut up and keep pushing."

Kathy herself wrote of her doubts that first day: *If the wind blew at this intensity all the time, our journey would be impossible, or unspeakably grim. Already I hated it. I hated the wind, I hated Tierra del Fuego, and I was angry at Réanne. "You really are stupid," I thought to myself. "You could be on the beach in Hawaii with a mai tai and a good book."*

"Shut up," said a voice from the other side of my head. "That's not you, Katherine."

But which was "me?" It was awful trying to move the damned bike with 40 pounds of gear down a gravel road. And we were to do this for 300 miles? We had to keep our heads down and couldn't even look around. "Masochist," I muttered to myself.

Kathy added later, in a journal article, that my dream had started out in reality as a "raging nightmare"[12]—another irony on her part, given that I had titled my 1994 book about Don's and my 1975 sailing adventure, *Cape*

Horn: One Man's Dream, One Woman's Nightmare.[13] Perhaps Kathy was already imagining the sequel: *Tierra del Fuego: One Woman's Dream, Another Woman's Nightmare?*

Wind, in any case, was to become for both of us almost a third "companion" on our trip, and its constant presence is one of the defining characteristics of Tierra del Fuego. In simple terms, this is because at mid-latitudes cold air travelling north from Antarctica encounters warm air from the equator and then swirls freely around the Southern Hemisphere, gaining energy without much hindrance from continental land masses. Tierra del Fuego also happens to be at the exact point where air and water currents of the Pacific Ocean meet those of the Atlantic. The turbulence is further exacerbated by the ramp-like presence of the southern Andes.

Bruce Chatwin described the region's winds as "stripping men to the raw."[14] He meant the winds would expose their souls, but it was easy for Kathy and me to imagine that without our wind-suits the flesh could be flayed from our bones.

Lucas Bridges, in his memoir *The Uttermost Part of the Earth*, contributes a legend from the Ona Indians about the Tierra del Fuegian winds.[15] According to the Ona, the four great winds were originally men. Naturally they had to know which of them was the strongest, so they held a wrestling contest. *Wintekhaiyin*, the east wind was persistent but far too gentle and was repeatedly overthrown by the others. *Orroknhaiyin*, the south wind, was fierce and strong, but he too was eventually overpowered. In the final, decisive contest, *Hechuknhaiyin*, the north wind was cunning, powerful and bad-tempered, but was forced to concede defeat to the inexhaustible west wind, *Kenenikhaiyin*. As Bridges noted, this myth elegantly encapsulates the characteristics of the four winds: *Wintekhaiyin*, the east wind blows moderately on summer mornings when the others are sleeping or resting, or until the north wind, *Hechuknhaiyin*, rouses himself. This wind blusters around, behaving badly until the west wind, *Kenenikhaiyin* arrives, at which time *Hechuknhaiyin* withdraws. *Orroknhaiyin* saves his strength for the winter, when the others are resting, and arrives in full force bringing snow.

This story made perfect sense to Kathy and me as we struggled on against the gusts. Of course the winds were unruly men, doing their utmost to make our lives difficult!

Five miles out of Porvenir, the route turned south so the wind now came at us from the side. With a little practice we were able to ride, maneuvering as if in a sailboat with the wind abeam. It was difficult at first, like heavy weather sailing, keeping the sails full, controlling the tiller and, above all, avoiding a knock down. But we soon caught on.

Two miles on, we passed a lake with *cisnes cuello negro* (black-necked swans) en masse, then little cygnets bobbing up and down alongside. I remembered the swans from our first visit to Porvenir in 1975. The mayor had taken Don and me on a driving tour of the town's environs, including a large lake to the north, Lago de los Cisnes (Lake of the Swans), where we had seen these birds, together with hundreds of flamingos. The sun, at just the right angle, lit up the birds in a panorama of pink, orange and blue—a gorgeous sight. At that time it was the beginning of the austral winter. The mayor told us that the swans usually left in winter, just as the flamingos were arriving. That year the flamingos had come early—nature's indication of a long hard winter to come. Don and I believed him! We had awakened on countless mornings to find ice on our deck, snowflakes in the air.

Now, it was February—mid-summer, though it hardly felt like it in the wind. I told Kathy that if we saw any flamingos on this trip, we were in trouble!

Another few miles on, we passed a former Salesian monastery that was

Black-necked swans.

now an agricultural school. This was one of several Salesian establishments on Isla Grande—a legacy of the days when missionaries had attempted to save the souls of the Fuegian Indians. (We would pass another monastery a few days later, south of Río Grande.)

Kathy's diary: *Because we were exerting ourselves so much and not taking in as much liquid as we should, we seldom needed to pee. But somewhere along the road that first day nature called. As a little departure gift, a friend had given me a blue plastic device that looked like a misshapen funnel, called the "Ladies Pal." Theoretically you could use it to pee standing up. "Let's try it," I thought.*

I went into a clump of bushes for privacy, pulled down my wool cycling shorts and underwear, but I wasn't able to spread my legs very wide. I did my best to position the blue "Pal" where I thought the pee would go, and gingerly let the urine flow. Immediately, I could feel the warm fluid running down my thigh. I stopped the stream, squatted, pitched the "Pal" aside and completed my business. I tried one further time with similar results, then tossed the silly thing in the trash. And even if it had worked, I would still

30

have had to take my pants down to my knees and stand there exposed to the whole world. Men may pee up a tree, but we girls are doomed to squat.

The road beyond the school followed a wild beach. The waves sweeping in across Paso Boquerón, were heavy at first. In the distance, across the water, we saw snowy peaks and a headland—Cabo Froward, the southernmost tip of the South American mainland. Named by the pirate Thomas Cavendish in 1587, "froward" in sixteenth-century English meant "adverse" or "unfavorable." When Don and I had limped past it in *Le Dauphin* in 1975, we thought it deserved its name; the fog hanging over it made it look forbidding and gloomy. But it also marked a literal turning point for us. Don had dashed below decks to fetch a bottle of Scotch and a cup. "Here, take a swig," he said to me. "We've got to toast the bloody south end of the Andes!"

I reflected now that Cabo Froward was as far south as Don would "accompany" me on my bicycle trip. From this point onwards, I was venturing into new territory. I would have no more memories of our 1975 trip to call forth. I drank an imaginary toast to the creation of new ones.

Kathy and I continued south on our bicycles, following the stretch along the western shore of the Straits known as "Tierra de la Luna," as it was full of craters studded with golf-ball-sized rocks. The road then curved around into a large bay, Bahía Inútil (Useless Bay), where the waters were more protected than those of the Strait. The road surface changed, too, from gravel to hard dirt road. We found this easier to ride on, even as we confronted potholes, washboards, rocks. Downhill runs were a particular challenge. We had to scan ahead for rocks and potholes while keeping a sharp eye directly in front of us. It was mentally tiring, as it required extreme concentration, and we were both timid at first, letting our bikes

South of Porvenir.

control us. ("Shift up, shift up," Don used to coach me going downhill. "Pedal so you get up momentum." My own head said otherwise: "I can't, it's too dangerous on this road.") But Kathy and I quickly realized we wouldn't get far unless we trusted ourselves to jump the hurdles. My hands ached from gripping and braking. "Riding roads like this is like riding a motocross bike," I thought. "Thank God for fat tires!"

Visually, this first full day of cycling was an impressionistic dream: geometric green hills, stream-carved ravines, turf thick with clover and chamomile, glacier-honed peaks stepping off towards Antarctica. My diary adds: *A glacial blue lake. Wild geese. A small coyote-like animal with black markings and a pointed nose.[16] A scarlet-breasted bird with black back and wings and a white stripe above the eyes. Wild canaries, some green, some yellow. The terrain reminded me of California's central coast—low mountains with deep, green ravines. Air redolent with clover smelled fresh and clean. Daisies, goldenrod, Queen Anne's lace covered the hills. A few trees here and there. Cars or trucks about every 10-15 minutes. Trucks hauling huge loads, possibly wool.*

The afternoon was warm (65°F) and we shed our touring jackets once we got out of the heavy winds. *"Cuatro estaciones en cada día"* ("four seasons in every day") was the saying at these latitudes. Don and I had experienced it numerous times in Punta Arenas, and it was no different here. One moment Kathy and I were riding in brilliant sunshine; five minutes later the sky would blacken, the temperature would plummet, and rain or sleet would pound us. Wool jerseys, windsuits, Gore-Tex pants and jackets came on and off with the rhythm of a revolving door.

About 20 miles from Porvenir we passed a sign: *Los Canales*. Assuming it was the entrance to an *estancia*, I went to examine a sign that I thought would give the names of the resident families. However, *Los Canales* was actually a campsite built in memory of one of the citizens of Porvenir. It was situated within a lovely little canyon with trees and shrubs, a stream, picnic tables, and fire pits big enough to barbecue a sheep (of which there were many grazing freely nearby). We pitched our Alpenlite Bivy II tent and took some water from the creek, boiling it and adding purifying tablets because it looked like muskeg water. We then enjoyed a meal of brown-tinted macaroni and cheese, with peas and a bacon bar, followed by pear strips, and a tot of rum each. We were both very tired but the setting was beautiful, our camp was cozy, and we were happy to have cycled even twenty miles, after starting the day thinking we might have to stay in Porvenir.

Kathy's final comment on the day: *"Lordy," I thought as I began to relax and enjoy the rum. "This morning was a nightmare. But things are looking up. We're camped in a comfortable little park a million miles from home, enjoying the long twilight and the smell of vanilla from one of the local trees. Canelo in Spanish."*

My own diary adds: *Geese honking overhead; 9:45 p.m. and still light. Lovely pink clouds off to the south. Perhaps this crazy trip is doable after all?*

Making supper.

CHAPTER 2

Tuesday, January 31: A miserable day, according to my diary: *First part beautiful on awful road. Second half monotonous and rainy, though on better roads. Couldn't find any place to camp with water nearby, so we dry-camped. We used our 1.5 quarts of bottled water to make soup: two packets chicken, the rest of the peas, one packet beef.*

The night was miserable too, with more rain that pounded on our tent at times. Neither of us slept very well.

Wednesday, February 1: The weather on this day was no better. Wind drove rain in horizontal sheets across unbroken pampa for much of our way. Cold gray Bahía Inútil looked as useless as its name. Streams were infrequent and we were becoming puffy-eyed from wind and dehydration. My head and body ached and I felt slightly nauseated. In spite of the rain in my face I could not get enough to drink. The landscape was monotonous, dreary, absolutely solitary and treeless—bleak, bleak, bleak.

Worst of all was the road. An all-dirt section had become a bog after all the rain. Kathy's journal tells the story: *Mud started to clog my tires. I whizzed through a couple of puddles thinking it would help clean them. Wrong! Suddenly the road deteriorated into a two-lane ribbon of dung. My bike sank in like a knife. One turn of the cranks and the wheels picked up two inches of mud. Forks filled up. Sprockets filled up. Came to a dead halt. I got off and tried to push it to the side of the road. G. D. thing would not budge. Took Réanne and me both to drag it. She bogged down, too, but not as badly. Thirty minutes of scraping before we could go on. Then I sank in again! More scraping. If I'd had a towel I'd have thrown it in right there. I wanted to kick the bike and myself. I wanted out of there, wanted to be clean and warm. Kept wondering what the hell I was doing there instead of on Maui sipping that Mai Tai, smelling frangipani. Let's hear it for karma! Réanne managed to stay afloat after the first stretch of mush—maybe because she was more careful, maybe because her tread isn't as deep. I was mad because I was having so much more trouble than she was,*

35

glad because she was staying calm, helping me out.[17]

We sat under a bridge for a rest and for a little protection from yet another downpour. The map showed us to be at a place called Puerto Nuevo, where some ruins and an old pier jutted out into the gray bay.

A pick-up truck—the first vehicle we had seen that day—stopped above us. The driver stuck his head out the window. "Need any help?" We asked if he had any drinking water. He didn't but offered to put the bikes in his truck and take us to the oil drilling camp at Onaisin, near the Argentine border.

Kathy looked at me. I hesitated, recalling my doubts from the first evening. But the purist in me found resolve. "No, we want to cycle all the way." We thanked the driver and asked how far to the next *estancia.*

"Seven miles. You'll find water there. Norwegians, are you?"

We laughed. Nobody had pegged us yet. "Americans," we said.

"Ah, I should have known. The only women brave enough to do this."

Pushing through the mud.

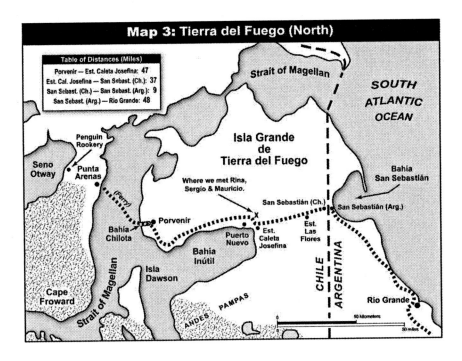

Map 3: Tierra del Fuego (North)

Brave or foolish? We climbed back onto our bicycles and pedaled on. By this time it was around noon. The truck driver's "seven miles" would get us to the end of Bahía Inútil, but I was growing increasingly concerned about the lack of water. We hoped there might be an *estancia* closer, where we could stop, sleep, wash, and so forth. But there was nothing. Nothing but mud, rain, a few cars and trucks passing.

We sighted a lake but couldn't tell whether it was an inlet of the sea or not, until I noticed a creek flowing into it. I volunteered to hike down and get water. The lake was about a mile away across the "moors." It was very boggy near the edge and there were sheep turds everywhere. The water was fresh, however, so I set about filling our bottles. White swans and black-neck swans floating on the lake objected to my presence, honking at me relentlessly until, mission completed, I walked back to the road. I was off course and called for Kathy. When I finally saw her, she said, "Where the hell have you been?"

"It's a hell of a long way down there," I snapped, piqued that she didn't appreciate what I'd done. She had stopped a truck and asked the driver if there were an *estancia* nearby where we could stop and get water.

"Two miles," he told her. "Estancia Fela."

We found the gate to Estancia Fela and were about to go through it when a red four-wheel-drive Toyota pick-up truck came down the road and stopped beside us. It was Sergio, Mauricio and Rina! They had told us they would be coming to Tierra del Fuego, but I hadn't really expected to see them, and I didn't recognize them at first. They regaled us with fresh bread, sausage, and bottles of 7-Up. We were still standing at the gate talking when the owners of Estancia Fela drove in. Sergio told us we should not follow them but instead continue along the road for a few more miles to another *estancia,* the Estancia Caleta Josefína, where we would find not only water but the possibility of sleeping in beds for the night. This would be a welcome end to the day. The *estancias* were not hotels or resorts, we knew, but some might still provide passing travelers like us with a place to stay.

A welcome surprise: Sergio, Rina and Mauricio, with Kathy.

Sergio, Mauricio and Rina left us with the remnants of the sausage, more bread, mangoes, bananas, and a bottle of pisco sour. Despite our protestations, they insisted we take it all, and we did after Sergio found a stowage place beneath the bungie on my bike.

Three miles down the road we came to the turnoff for Estancia Caleta Josefína, at the head of Bahía Inútil. We started down the side-road and a nice-looking young man, about 30, with dark hair, stopped to ask where we were going. Kathy asked him if it was possible to get water and a place to sleep at the *estancia*. He told her to ask for Don Tomás, which we did.

Don Tomás turned out to be a man in his late sixties, tall, lean, weather-beaten with one blind eye. He directed us to his house, told us to bring our bikes to his yard, then showed us where there was a faucet and hose next door. His house was well made and cute, like one built in 1920s America. Don Tomás left us there and went back to his work. We went about washing off the mud, scraping and cleaning. An *ovejero* (shepherd) with rosy cheeks came out and asked us in for tea. We thanked him and said we'd be in after we finished our cleaning. A fresh sheepskin hung on a drying frame above where Kathy was washing her bags. We went in for tea and were offered coffee instead, good and hot, along with delicious, freshly made yeast bread.

Three other people sat at the tea table, all men, very taciturn. Kathy and I did most of the talking. Two of the men were drinking *maté*; the third, who was reading a sheep-ranching magazine, *Ovina*, seemed better educated than the other two. The only questions they asked were where we were going, where we were from, and where we had slept the night before.

Don Tomás had asked us if we would like fresh eggs for supper. I cooked one and it tasted wonderful. Kathy and I ate it with freeze-dried curried rice and "chicken with cashews" that had no chicken in it.

Don Tomás came back to the house after having supper with his crew of sheep shearers. He lit the gas lights in the kitchen and turned on two stove burners to create some heat for us. He told us he had spent 20 years as a rancher near Río Gallegos, in southern Argentina, but he was born on Tierra del Fuego and had been at Estancia Caleta Josefína for three years. There were no women on the ranch, so he did all his own housework. While we were there, he ran around cleaning up, mopping the bathroom floor, emptying the trash, cleaning the toilet, etc. He invited us to watch the sheep-shearing before we left the next day. How did they decide which sheep were used for wool and which were killed for meat? Don Tomás replied that they used the best animals for wool and the "poor" ones for slaughter. There was a freezing facility (*frigorífico*) in Porvenir. The *estancia* had 5,000 sheep in all, and they sheared 200 animals a day—the entire process taking about two and a half weeks, after which the crew of shearers moved to another *estancia*.

Kathy and I were surprised to find a military compound on the *estancia*, and soldiers playing basketball till almost midnight. Why were they here? Don Tomás didn't know. He shrugged his shoulders as if to say, I wonder myself. "*Siempre así,*" he said. "It's always been this way."

Thursday, February 2: Up at 7 a.m. after a good night's sleep in a good bed. Breakfast of cocoa and an orange, which Sergio and Rina had given us. Kathy and I packed our gear, then I spent an hour doing bike maintenance, trying to adjust the derailleur (gear changer) on my bicycle.

I gave up and joined Kathy, who was watching the men shearing sheep, which was done in a shed with electric shears. The shearer started on the sheep's belly, then progressed to its back. There was a real art to it, and some shearers were better than others. Some wore hats like nets to keep their hair out of their face. The sheep were afraid but once they were grabbed they didn't resist. They truly were "lambs going to slaughter."

Estancia Caleta Josefina and gauchos.

In the shearing shed.

The wool was gathered in one piece, rolled and packed into large cloth bales, then the men jumped up and down until the bales were as full as possible. After that they used a wool press machine to pack them down even more. Once full, the bales were wrapped, sealed and sent to Punta Arenas for shipping.

Pablo, the young man we had met the previous day on the track into Caleta Josefína, returned as Kathy and I were preparing to leave. He explained that Don Tomás was an uncle of his father, who had been the proprietor of the *estancia*. Pablo's father had died the previous year and his mother, who lived in Santiago, had no interest in sheep ranching, so Pablo had become the proprietor. The *estancia* was 80 years old but it had been divided many times and was now only (*only!*) 12,500 acres in size. Pablo loved the land, but he was trained in civil engineering and was unsure if he wanted to live on the *estancia*. He was a sensitive, well-spoken young man.

Pablo loaded our bikes and equipment into his truck and drove us from the *estancia* to the main road to save us from having to maneuver through the mud again. According to our map it was 28 miles to Estancia Las Flores, a place Sergio and Rina had mentioned before we left Punta Arenas. They knew the *dueña*, an elderly woman, and had given Kathy and me a letter of introduction. We figured we could get there that day, 1) if it didn't rain, 2) if there was no wind, and 3) if the road was good. All were big "ifs" that had not happened so far.

As it turned out, we had absolutely marvelous conditions, with a hard dirt road and the wind behind us for the first (and only!) time on our trip. By the end of the day we had "flown" 36 miles—our greatest mileage since the start. And we had achieved it in spite of ongoing problems with my bike. The derailleur had come off and broken a spoke, which I wired to another spoke because I couldn't remove the broken one. Shifting to higher gears was now impossible. I told myself repeatedly that it was "absolutely insane" to have come without a change of chain and clusters, but I felt good and pedaled hard and steadily. Meanwhile, Kathy fairly flew, spurred on by the magic combination of sunshine, a tailwind and a decent road. ("It was pure elation," she wrote later, "A narcotic after three days of grinding along the stony road against cold wind."[18]) I could not keep up with her and speculated that even with a better bike I probably wouldn't have been able to do so. Clearly, all Kathy's worries about training had been in vain!

Though we had not left Estancia Caleta Josefína until late morning, we reached Estancia Las Flores at 3:30 p.m. The 28 miles had taken so little time we could hardly believe we had arrived at the same Las Flores Sergio and Rina had told us about. No wonder they urged us to visit. Its name was fitting—the house was surrounded by a beautiful flower garden, with wild roses, giant lupine, snapdragons and a grass lawn. The *dueña*, La Nonna, was an 81-year-old widow who possessed a wonderfully warm sense of humor and a hearty laugh. She had emigrated to Tierra del Fuego from Yugoslavia as a young bride, and she and her husband were among the early settlers of the land. Sixty years later, she was still managing her small sheep ranch, directing and feeding her crew of workers, caring for her garden, and greeting passers-by from all parts of the world—Kathy and me included— with grandmotherly hugs. Sergio and Rina had visited her the day before and told her about our impending arrival. She served us tea with homemade bread, rhubarb jam, fresh butter and tea. Kathy and I scarfed down three pieces each. Then we signed her guest book. Dating from 1968, it included the names of all the people who had stopped by the house over the years. There were signatures from four other cyclists—one Japanese, two French ("Alain *et* Babette"), and a German.

Las Flores had a notably feminine touch that was lacking in other places, such as Caleta Josefína, where no women were in residence. La Nonna was one of the few ranch women on the Chilean side of Tierra del

La Nonna (with friend), Estancia Las Flores.

Fuego. But, understandably, young *Chilenas* had no desire to try the pioneer life, preferring an easier existence in towns, where they were within reach of their families.

We thanked La Nonna for her hospitality and rode on towards the towns of San Sebastián. I write "towns"—plural—because there is one on each side of the Chilean-Argentine border. The Chilean San Sebastián was little more than a *carabinero* station, occupying some old *estancia* buildings a couple of miles before the actual border. Although we had pedaled uphill at times from Las Flores, the road from Chilean San Sebastián onwards was mostly downhill, traversing a huge plain that tilted like a wedge toward the Atlantic. Pink foxgloves colored a landscape unbroken by tree, house or hill. There was more sky than land and a 360-degree horizon. Kathy observed, "Anyone who lived here would think the earth was a disk." Indeed, it shone like silver in the late-afternoon light, the sky above a lapis dome with mounded clouds.

Glorious weather and a decent road on the way to San Sebastián. Neither was to last.

CHAPTER 2

Our bodies were one with the bicycles, our riding skills honed on rocks and pot holes. We steamed along at top speed, whooping, confident that, except for mud, we could ride any road—including the one we were on. Between Chilean San Sebastián and its Argentine counterpart nine miles further on, the road changed horribly—a no man's land that neither country attempted to maintain. But we had ridden worse. Meanwhile, the Argentine landscape appeared to have been scraped clean. No trees, shrubs or plants. Mist hung low as we approached the colorless Atlantic. Gray mudflats stretched along the horizon at low tide, dotted by shorebirds pecking for bite-sized mollusks. But our spirits remained high. In five hours we had cycled twice the distance of our first two days.

The second San Sebastián was a dusty hamlet on the Atlantic shore, comprised of little more than a gas station, a small *hostería*, and the Argentine border station. Kathy and I had to show our papers to the Argentine authorities, who were not very friendly at first, but warmed up as we talked. Then Kathy and I had the pleasure of sleeping once again on proper beds, at the San Sebastián Auto Club Hostería.

Friday, February 3: At the end of this day I complained to my diary that *each day seems like a week. So many things happened yesterday I can't remember whether they really happened yesterday, the day before or two days before.* And this day, too, was eventful:

We left the *hostería* in San Sebastián around 10 a.m. To the reader this might sound leisurely, but it took us two to three hours every morning to repack our gear—sleeping bags, clothes, camping gear—then mount our bags on the bikes, etc. It was much more laborious than backpacking, and we usually had bike maintenance to do also.

Our friends Sergio and Rina had remarked favorably on the roads in Argentine Tierra del Fuego. For the first hour out of San Sebastián, we

47

shared their opinion—we were going up and down a lot, but the road was wide and cambered and the surface was fairly good. Too good to last! Suddenly, my God, it was "paved," not with gravel, but with fist-size rocks packed into the dirt. The effect was a sort of "natural" cobblestone, as if the sky had rained rocks that all stuck on the road. They jolted our backs necks and hands and made us wonder if our bikes would hold together. Rain had damaged the road in places as well, and the *Departmento Nationale de Vehiculos* (DNV) was out with its road grader. The banks were carved and so steep in some places that I found it hard to maneuver.

"Natural" cobblestones.

Even so, we moved along at a fairly good pace. By 1 p.m. we had ridden at least 20 miles, but our sense of humor was sagging so we stopped for lunch. The temperature was 68°F and the sun felt like a balm on our tired muscles. Then, suddenly, the warmth evaporated. "Look how fast those clouds are moving," I remarked to Kathy. The sky clotted with darkness. Hail began to fall as we scrambled to pack up. A furious head wind came up, and the hail turned into glacially cold rain.

A surreal quality prevailed for the next few hours. Black sky, then blue, then black again. Intermittent bursts of sun. Multiple rainbows. Dark clouds warred for a chance to dump on us, while white ones funneled to the ground in thin wisps. We rode on for another hour. Unable to make enough headway, we got off and pushed. I fell on my knee while trying to make room for a passing truck and for several minutes I couldn't move for the pain. Then, at what seemed like the peak of our misery, we came onto pavement, the first since Porvenir. With this road we could make it to Río

Pavement! And more hail headed our way.

49

Grande by dinnertime. Three miles later, the pavement ended. Back to cobblestone. Our short-lived respite had come courtesy of the Argentine government, which had paved a short stretch to use as an airstrip during the Falklands (Malvinas) War two years earlier.

Kathy: *My hands were so numb I could barely bend my fingers. My speech slurred because my face was frozen. My brain felt equally numb. Réanne and I had been pushing through sleet and rain that slammed us from an angle. Although we'd been pushing as hard as we could, we were making little progress. Visibility was near zero. Réanne couldn't talk either, and I would not have been able to hear her above the howl of the wind anyway. I didn't know how much farther it was to Río Grande but began to doubt if either of us had the strength to get there in this weather.*

By mid-afternoon the wind was lashing harder and we had to push the bikes again. We had made just nine miles since lunch. Reaching Río Grande that day would be impossible. But camping out was not an option either. We scanned the limited horizon for an *estancia*. Nothing. Fifteen miles still to go. As a double trailer-truck passed us going north, we turned our backs against the frigid blast of air and to avoid flying rock and mud. The truck stopped a couple of hundred yards down the road, then backed up slowly until it reached us. Rolling the window down and gesturing toward the sky, the driver shouted in Spanish, "What are you doing out here?"

"Riding to Ushuaia," we answered, in Spanish, like children—or lunatics.

"Flag down a truck and get the hell to town!" he commanded in a big-brotherly tone. "There's nothing between here and Río Grande. You can't survive out here!"

"*Gracias,*" Kathy and I shouted in unison as he closed his window and drove off. We looked at each other. Kathy looked terrible and I knew I looked worse. We were both soaked and shivering, on the verge of hypothermia, if not frostbite. The driver was right. Kathy decided he was another angel of mercy, commandeering us to do what we hadn't the sense to figure out for ourselves. We wanted to ride every inch of the road to Ushuaia, but purism had strayed into stupidity.

We held our blue-gloved thumbs high as the next truck approached, promising ourselves that we would try to ride the 15-mile section between there and Río Grande on our bike-bus-hitchhike return trip.

A pick-up truck driven by a young oilman took pity on us. He drove us for thirty minutes, then blew a tire. He radioed for another to be brought from Río Grande. We sat for an hour and a half as rain continued intermittently.

To pass the time, we talked about the Falklands (Malvinas) War, fought between Argentina and Britain two years earlier. Both countries claim rights to the Falklands Islands (Islas Malvinas), an archipelago in the South Atlantic 300 miles east of Tierra del Fuego. Argentina claims the islands on geographical grounds, though Britain has administered the Falklands, together with South Georgia and the South Sandwich Islands, as a Crown Colony since 1841. The 1982 war had been triggered by an unauthorized landing on South Georgia of a party of Argentine "scrap metal salvagers," who provocatively raised their nation's flag. This incident rapidly escalated into what the writer Simon Winchester called "Britain's very last Imperial war."[19] Britain's then-Prime Minister, Margaret Thatcher, and Argentina's ruling military junta, led by General Leopoldo Galtieri, both saw it as an opportunity to gain political capital—and indeed, Thatcher, as leader of the victorious side, was re-elected the following year, while the junta in Argentina was overthrown. The war lasted for 74 days, from April 2 to June 14, 1982, with hundreds of casualties on both sides and several thousand wounded, along with a number of sunken ships and no lasting resolution to the dispute: Britain retains sovereignty of the Falklands to this day, but claims to the islands are included in Argentina's constitution.

The driver of the pick-up told us that he had been opposed to the war. This seemed to be true of most people Kathy and I talked to in Tierra del Fuego. The island was not just physically detached from the rest of Argentina, it was politically removed as well. The driver said that a lot of young people from the mainland came to Tierra del Fuego to avoid being conscripted.

The truck tire eventually arrived, and by 6:30 p.m. we were in Río Grande, standing at the reception desk of the Hotel Los Yaganes. This was an upmarket establishment by Tierra del Fuegian standards, the biggest and best hotel in town. The manager's pomaded black hair, starched white shirt and impeccably tailored suit made me suddenly conscious of my appearance—mud and grease on my bright yellow Gore-Tex rain suit, bags under my eyes, hair damp and matted. "*You* ask for a room," I directed Kathy. "I'll go watch the bikes." I felt like the Michelin Man in my five layers of outer wear. With Kathy's navy Gore-Tex jacket, blond braids and slightly cleaner royal blue rain pants, I thought she'd have more success.

"I'm sorry, we're *todo completo*," the manager told Kathy. Totally full. And no, he didn't know what other hotels to suggest. There were two others in Río Grande, and they, too, were usually "*completo*" by that hour on Fridays.

We checked the other hotels on foot. Same story. Back to Los Yaganes. We discussed alternatives: sitting in the lobby all night, or even getting drunk and disorderly. The prospect of spending the night in jail appealed to us more than pitching a tent in the rain in the bleak countryside around Río Grande.

Our desperation must have showed. A well-dressed Argentine who'd been watching us came over. "You couldn't find any rooms in town?" he asked. "Let me talk to the manager for you."

Suddenly and mysteriously a cancellation occurred. "One night only," the manager cautioned. That was all we wanted. We thanked the Argentine profusely for his kind intervention. "Another angel to add to the list," Kathy said. Neither of us was religious, but I agreed with her. "But for the kindness of strangers. . ."

Then another difficulty arose. The Los Yaganes manager wouldn't accept traveler's checks or Visa. The banks were closed until Monday and there were no *cambios* (money exchange offices) in town.

"Look," the manager said in exasperation, "I need to pay my *National Geographic* subscription in U.S. dollars. You pay it when you get back to the States and I'll cover the room." We agreed (and I did pay the subscription after our return to California). Then, smiling, we asked where we could park our muddy bicycles. The manager did not smile in return, but he led us to a storage closet.

For entertainment that evening, we attended a slide-show at the hotel given by Jorge Damián Flores, a local photographer. Afterwards, a man approached us, addressing us as "*chicas*," and invited us to have breakfast with him the next morning. He wasn't being chivalrous—breakfast came with the price of the room—but he was interested in our story. We found that educated people were keen to ask us questions, whereas "ordinary" workers (the pick-up truck driver; a man waiting on the side of the road for a bus) just seemed to accept us as part of the scenery—or else as people who had dropped in from the moon.

Saturday, February 4: Before leaving the hotel we telephoned the Auto Club Hostería in Ushuaia to book a room for later in the week. Again, "*completo*." We would have to wing it when we got there.

Back on the road at 10 a.m. Cold and windy. Kathy put on four sweaters. I wore my wind suit. Fifteen miles south of Río Grande, there was a demarcation line as trees reappeared: beech with delicate green leaves, trimmed with yellow-green lichen like witches' hair—windblown and unkempt. Streams tumbled from the last peaks of the Andes becoming rivers that cut patterns across grassy valleys on their way to the Atlantic.

Drinking water and sheltered camping spots would no longer be a problem. The road and my bike were. I ached all over and could use only my three lowest gears. Cleaning, lubing, adjusting made no improvement. The other fifteen gears were unavailable. For every stroke Kathy made, I needed three. I couldn't keep up and began to feel sorry for myself, playing the "should" dialogue: "I should have changed my cluster before we left (well, you didn't, so quit thinking about it). I should be able to keep up (you can't, so don't worry about it). It was my idea to come here, I should be leading (what a dumb idea; this isn't a race. Face it, you're slower. Keep pedaling and enjoy what you can.)"

I should have changed my cluster before we left.

54

CHAPTER 2

Kathy was engaged in her own inner dialogue: *"Jesus Christ, at this rate we won't get to Ushuaia till Christmas... Come on, Réanne, hurry up... She's the ultimate planner. How could she not have her bike in good shape? Why didn't she get a new derailleur before we left home? We're doing this trip and there's not a bike store for a thousand miles... Hurry up, Réanne, crank harder... But she can't, poor woman. And nor is she likely to give up. We're in this together. My only option is to be patient... And it's not all bad. It's exhilarating to be able to attack a steep hill in low gear and steam right up it like nothing. I can feel the strength in my thigh muscles: body and bike a well-oiled machine. I feel like I could ride to the end of the earth. Actually, I am riding to the end of the earth! Come on, Réanne..."*

At some point during the afternoon we stopped at a service station and bought fuel for our stove. We camped that night in a *bosque* (wood). Our stove did not work very well with the Argentine gasoline, which evaporated immediately when priming, then flared up into a bonfire (Tierra del Fuego indeed!). Eventually I managed to heat water for soup, and Kathy and I both slept extremely well on soft, mossy ground beneath low-canopied beech trees.

Setting up camp.

Sunday, February 5: Light rain fell during the night, and by the time we had breakfast, wind and sun had dried the tent. We spent the usual two hours packing up, then set out. The road was abominable. More cobblestones. We followed the coast with not much change in scenery until Río Ewan, where we stopped to fill our water bottles. Forty-five miles south of Río Grande, Río Ewan was little more than a river crossing and a police station. A young policeman appeared and told us the river water was *sucio* (dirty), and that we should come to the police station to get water. Kathy had sunk in mud up to her ankles trying to get to the clean water and had mud flowing into her shoes. The young policeman seemed glad of the diversion. He lived alone in this remote place and was very polite and kind. Kathy and I reflected that policemen of both nationalities had been very nice to us in Tierra del Fuego so far.

Sergio, Mauricio, and Rina passed by in the late morning, on their way home to Punta Arenas, and stopped to chat. They had with them the young granddaughter of La Nonna, of Estancia Las Flores, who told us she'd been hearing our story all along the way. Sergio and Rina invited us to come back to their house when we made it back to Punta Arenas.

Lunch was a fat red sausage that Rina and Sergio gave us and was more edible than it looked. Kathy and I were sitting at the side of the road eating when the man who had approached us after the slide-show in Río Grande drove by, honked, stopped and got out to ask how we were doing and when we were returning to Río Grande. (We had declined to have breakfast with him, but he did not seem to be affronted.)

The "devil's cobblestones" continued for the rest of the day. We had no choice but to endure. Thank goodness we had slept well! Our goal for the day was the Hostería Kaiken, at the near end of a long fjord-like lake, Lago Fagnano. We were still struggling on at 6 p.m. when we passed a saw mill. There were quite a few of these in the southern, forested part of

56

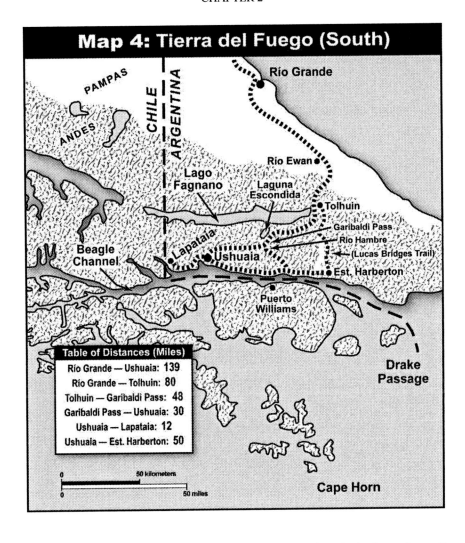

Map 4: Tierra del Fuego (South)

Table of Distances (Miles)
Río Grande — Ushuaia: 139
Río Grande — Tolhuin: 80
Tolhuin — Garibaldi Pass: 48
Garibaldi Pass — Ushuaia: 30
Ushuaia — Lapataia: 12
Ushuaia — Est. Harberton: 50

Isla Grande, with sawn beech and plywood as their principal products. I suggested to Kathy that we go in and ask someone for hot water so we could make soup. The entranceway was barred by an iron gate, like the boom gate at a railway crossing, locked with a huge chain and padlock. We tilted our bikes to get them under the gate and rode in. The first place we came to was a small bunkhouse near the road. A man came out and Kathy told him what we wanted. He had a small round woodstove in the bunkhouse, along with two beds and a table. He invited us in and set a kettle on to boil. Kathy and I dripped with sweat—it was hot in the bunkhouse and we were dressed in multiple layers of cycling clothes. When the water was ready we prepared our instant soup (green pea flavor with an added bacon bar) and stayed for the next hour. The man told us there were 40 workers at the mill, all Chilenos. They earned 4,500 pesos a month (equivalent to US$125, or $1,500 a year), room and board were supplied.

Our host was Chilean also, originally from Puerto Montt though he had worked for years in Río Gallegos, on the southern Argentine mainland. He was dark and swarthy, with a handsome nose and thick facial skin, as though he had spent a lifetime outside. He told us another cyclist had passed by about a month before (the German in La Nonna's guest book) and had eaten dinner with the millworkers, after stopping first at the small bunkhouse. Kathy suggested that he should put a sign over his door: *Casa de Cyclistas!*

As we left the sawmill property and started back on the main road, the slide-show man from Río Grande passed by again on his return trip north and gave us a cheerful wave. Tierra del Fuego felt like a small town. We kept running into the same people and everybody seemed to know everybody else.

The man at the bunkhouse had told us there was a store only two miles down the road, at the tiny hamlet of Tolhuin, where we could buy food. It was after 8 p.m. when we arrived. Kathy assumed they'd be closed because it was Sunday. I said, "If they're good business people, they'll be open; if they're normal Argentines they won't be." They were open. The store was tended by an old woman and a very short little man with a high squeaky voice. Both were very amiable. We bought some Edam cheese, crackers, cookies and Tang.

The Hostería Kaiken was still several miles down the road. Neither Kathy nor I had the energy to continue, so we made camp on the edge of

Tolhuin, beside a beaver dam on the Río Turbio. Beavers had become naturalized in Tierra del Fuego after fifty of the animals were introduced from Canada in 1946 in an attempt by the Argentine government to start a local fur industry. The trade never took off, and the beavers ran amok, turning whitewater streams into ponds and meadows. This was causing problems for Isla Grande sheep ranchers and some damage to backcountry roads and trails. But Kathy and I were grateful that night for the soft patch of beaver meadow on which we pitched our tent.

Monday, February 6: We awoke at 7 a.m. to rain. "Maybe it will go away if we sleep some more," Kathy said. Maybe. We slept for another hour and a half. The rain didn't stop. We took turns packing our gear inside the tent and getting dressed before facing the day. The tent was entirely soaked. It was miserable packing up and setting forth in the rain.

We left Río Turbio at 11 a.m. and arrived at the Hostería Kaiken a half hour later. It was a modern establishment, constructed by the government and administered, like the hotel in San Sebastián, by the Argentine Automobile Club. Kathy and I thought we might stay there for the day and dry out. No such luck. It was "*todo completo*." Of course. I asked the young man at the reception desk sarcastically what we were supposed to do. He assured me we'd find someplace to stay in Ushuaia. But Ushuaia was still 60 miles down the road. Kathy and I waited around, drinking coffee and eating day-old bread, hoping we might yet be able to get a room. A busload of Argentine tourists arrived. They were much interested in our cycling feats but of no practical help to us. It seemed to us that Tierra del Fuego was a little overwhelmed by the Argentine government's successful efforts to promote tourism in the region.

Natalie Goodall noted in her guidebook that 57,000 tourists visited Tierra del Fuego in the 1976-77 season (December-March), with more arriving every year. She wrote that the island was "hard pressed to handle such an influx of people."[20] That was Kathy's and my observation, too—though, of course, we were tourists ourselves.

At 1 p.m., we finally gave up on Hostería Kaiken and headed down the road. It was still raining. The road followed the long shoreline of Lago Fagnano. The sky cleared eventually and we cycled on, aiming to reach the point at which the road turned south from the lake, and where we thought there was another *hostería*. At 6 p.m. the rain was long gone, but the wind was blowing like hell and we were not making any headway. We stopped at a saw mill to ask about the *hostería*. "Five miles down the road." Two men told us there was another, much nicer *hostería* at Laguna Escondido. "We're going by there. We'll take you." They loaded us and our bikes into the back of their truck, and drove along the dirt road at 50 m.p.h. while Kathy and I clung to our bikes. We passed one *hostería*—the one we had been aiming for—and continued on so far we thought the men intended to drive us all the way to Ushuaia. Twenty minutes later we pulled into the Hostería Petrel, a pleasant-looking establishment with a dozen or so rooms on the shore of Laguna Escondida. The driver ran in to verify there was a room for us. A young señora, a friend of the driver, greeted us graciously, saying she had *habitación* for one night.

We were glad to have a place to stay, and the Hostería Petrel was very nice but not restful. The other tourists, all Argentines, were loud and abrasive. All of the women smoked, even those who looked too young to do so. Kids in dirty-stockinged feet ran up and down, screaming. Disco music played in the public areas, so loud that Kathy and I could barely hear one another talk. She and I had come to Tierra del Fuego, in part, for its raw, wild beauty and its remoteness—but on this night it was hard to convince ourselves that we had truly "gotten away from it all."

Kathy recorded her own, ongoing frustrations in her diary: *Before this misbegotten adventure, I had no idea how wearying wind could be. There were always the three of us: me, Réanne, and the goddamned wind, which was always blowing the wrong way, trying to push us back, to rob us of the precious mileage we had made. I hate the monotony of pushing the bike and its heavy panniers, of having to keep my head down against the endless blasts of wind. I couldn't imagine living in a place where it blew like this continuously. I would go mad. I might yet go mad before we get to Ushuaia—if we ever get to Ushuaia. I'll stick it out, but I will NEVER sign up to ride in a place like this again. Sometimes I feel like screaming 'stop it!' at the wind gods, as though they could hear my puny voice against the roar of their own. All day today it blew and blew, until I was blue, and it will blow again tomorrow. Of that we can be sure. A 30-to-40 mile-an-hour blow is on the menu every day. It's not for me!*

Tuesday, February 7: From Laguna Escondida, it was a short, twisting climb up to 1,419-foot Garibaldi Pass, the highest point of our entire 300-mile journey. Though the road surface was horrible, and I had not gotten much sleep, I managed the ascent well enough with my three low gears. The wind at the Pass was ferocious, but we stopped to admire the view back down to Laguna Escondida and, in the distance, Lago Fagnano.

After Garibaldi Pass, the ride turned into an interminable roller coaster that was pure hell. I tried several times to shift into a high gear to gain downhill momentum. Each time my chain spun off and into the rear wheel, the third time breaking another spoke. I used every obscenity I knew in three languages. Kathy had rounded a curve and was out of sight. I was furious. With myself, with the bike, with her. I contemplated the 200-yard drop at the edge of the road, wanting to shove the damn bike over it.

"What happened?" Kathy had left her bike and walked back to help. I pointed, too angry to speak. "Have a cookie," she said. "Let me work on it." She was the right person to have brought with me, I thought as I cooled down.

Above: Climbing up to Garibaldi Pass.

Below: A quick snack at the summit.

Kathy struggling to put on her wind suit, Garibaldi Pass.

Later, I learned Kathy had been having her own problems. She wrote in her diary: *We came to the Cordillera today, rosy mountain peaks and fern-soft beech forests, but I couldn't enjoy it much because of the road. On top of it all, one of my front racks snapped and bent above the screw hole. I ended up having to hang that pannier on the rear. Felt like I was riding a lopsided camel. Bouncing on that "cobblestone" made me twice as tired mentally and physically as other sections have done. "I hate this," I yelled to no one as I crested a long hill this afternoon. Réanne was lagging behind. I stopped to wait, but I wanted to go, to get through that section. "Hurry up, dammit," I commanded the tiny speck down the road. Then I told myself, "Cut it out; be glad you're not having to struggle so hard."*[21]

At dusk, after the long downhill run, the road surface changed from cobblestone to concrete. Kathy dismounted from her bike and kissed the pavement. We had reached the edge of Ushuaia—the southernmost city on earth. It had taken us nine days to get here on our bicycles from Porvenir. We had done what we set out to do—but what a letdown. We wanted a brass band and champagne for our arrival on bicycle at the end of the world, but the Fuegian weather gods served water. Torrential rain began at the outskirts of town, obscuring the postcard beauty of snow-covered peaks, beech forests, even the Beagle Channel. The sky seemed to have been storing it up just for our big moment.

Even worse, all the hotels were *"completo."* The quiet little town we'd read about, "halfway between an Alpine ski resort and a Canadian timber town,"[22] was full of Argentine tourists from Buenos Aires. Shops sold plastic penguins, ash trays made in Taiwan, even "I ♥ Ushuaia" bumper stickers. We were back in civilization but found it lonely compared to the Chilean side of the island, with its see-forever skies, clover-scented air, undulating hills and pampa, and its slow-paced people.

But, let it rain. We found what was surely the last room in town, available for one night only, but tomorrow would take care of itself.

Kissing the pavement, Ushuaia.

Ushuaia.

CHAPTER 3

HERO AND HARBERTON

Situated on the Beagle Channel, on the south shore of Isla Grande, and fringed by a rugged range of mountains to the north, Ushuaia is the capital of Argentine Tierra del Fuego. Its name, a Yahgan Indian word, means "a bay penetrating to the westward."

Ushuaia was founded by Anglican missionaries, who arrived in 1869 to civilize the Yahgans—the "canoe Indians" of the Beagle Channel area. One of the missionaries, a man named Thomas Bridges, learned the rich Yahgan language and compiled the only known English-Yahgan dictionary (now kept in the British Museum in London), as well as a Yahgan version of the New Testament. In 1888, as sheep ranchers established their *estancias* all over Isla Grande—to the detriment of the natives—Bridges relocated his mission from Ushuaia to an island near Cape Horn, where it endured until 1920. By that time, all of the remaining full-blood Yahgans had died.

Lucas Bridges, one of Thomas Bridges' five children, born in Ushuaia in 1875, lived among the last surviving natives and defended them publicly against the *estancia* owners. His 1949 memoir, *The Uttermost Part of the Earth*, tells in part of the struggle between the two cultures.

Ushuaia evolved from a mission station, to an Argentine navy base and convict settlement, to a modern city. When Kathy and I were there in 1984, its population was around 8,000. Thirty years later the city has grown to around 64,000. Natalie Goodall, a Ushuaian resident herself, wrote in

1979 that most of the city's inhabitants were employed in some way by official agencies, whether the Argentine Navy or various branches of government, including the National Park service. Many more now make a living from tourism. The city remains a naval port, and has become a busy departure point for cruise ships bound for the Antarctic and yachts headed to and from Cape Horn. Kathy and I found it busy enough already in 1984, compared to everywhere else we had been on Tierra del Fuego. Also, like every place else in Tierra del Fuego, it was windy. Though the early mornings were calm, as the day progressed the wind would come up and reach gale-force by mid-afternoon.

Wednesday, February 8: The Hotel Maiten, where Kathy and I had found a room the previous evening, could accommodate us for only one night. Since we planned to stay in Ushuaia for a few days, our first priority in the morning was to visit the tourist bureau to find another place to stay. The manager called six *casas de familias* before finding one with a room for us. The *dueña*, Señora Heidi Suarez, said she would meet us at 2 p.m. at the *Oficina de Turismo*. She arrived at 2:45 p.m., just as Kathy and I were about to set off to find our own way to her address. Señora Suarez took a taxi back to her house, carrying our bags with her while we cycled the rest of the way. She showed us a room with one bed. We figured one of us could sleep on the floor. Señora Suarez wouldn't hear of it. She said we could move a bed from the dining room into the bedroom. She was talkative to an extreme, but very friendly.

We washed our hair for the first time in five days. We also used, for the first time, the hair dryer Kathy had lugged in her bicycle panniers for the past 300 miles—the one item we had with us that required electricity. We had bought an adapter plug for it earlier in the day. Kathy had tried to explain what she needed and the owner of the store kept saying, "*No entiendo.* (I don't understand.)" I finally remembered the word *"prisa"* (plug). "Ah," he said, and reached right away for an adapter. Now we could dry our hair!

The other major item on Kathy's shopping list in Ushuaia was a pair of long pants. She was tired of having nothing to wear but her black wool cycling shorts, with only electric blue wind-pants to keep her legs warm. We went into a couple of stores and she ended up with a pair of brown denim jeans that she had to roll up because they were too long. But at least she had something to cover her legs that wasn't conspicuous.

Having accomplished that, there were two things I wanted to do in Ushuaia. Both were connected. The first was to meet Natalie Goodall, the American-born biologist and author who lived in Ushuaia. I had read her guidebook to Tierra del Fuego when I was planning the bicycle trip and had written to her before leaving the States. I was curious to meet her, but I was also hoping she could connect me with the crew of an Ushuaia-based Antarctic supply ship, the *Hero*. Don and I had been in regular radio contact with the *Hero* during our 1975 sailing voyage. The ship's radio operator, John, had been very helpful, patching us through to friends and family in the States, and he had been the last person we spoke to before our pitchpole. Natalie had a connection with the *Hero*, since she was associated with the U.S. Antarctic Research Program in Ushuaia. If the *Hero* was in port, perhaps Natalie could serve as my introduction.

I asked Señora Suarez if I could phone Natalie Goodall. She replied, "Go to her house, *no mas.*" She gave us directions and we cycled over. As we walked up to the door a dog shot out. Natalie Goodall herself appeared and called the dog. I introduced myself, then Kathy. Natalie said, "Just a minute, I have to telephone someone. When she came back, she invited us, somewhat coolly, to "Come in, if you want."

I told Natalie I'd written her. She replied that she had just received the letter. (I learned later she had been away in December at a conference in the States.) I had envisioned her as a shy, quiet American woman, collecting plants and doing the distinctive pen-and-ink drawings that feature in her guidebook. How presumptuous of me. She was a large and confident person, about my age and extremely busy with scientific research and writings. Originally from Ohio, she had worked as a biologist for an oil company and traveled extensively in South America, collecting and illustrating plants. Inspired by Lucas Bridges' book, *The Uttermost Part of the Earth*, she had visited Tierra del Fuego where she met her future husband, Thomas Goodall. He was Lucas Bridges' great-nephew and one of the owners of the Bridges family *estancia* at Harberton, on the Beagle Channel 50 miles east of Ushuaia.

I explained to Natalie that I wanted to contact Captain Pieter Lenie of the *Hero*. She walked over to her radio and called him, telling him we would like to visit him and his ship. He asked, "Are they at your house now?"

"Yes."

"I'll come right over and pick them up."

I asked Natalie if we could leave our bikes in her yard for the evening. She was more friendly now that she realized we were cyclists, and because of our connection with the *Hero*. She offered to pick us up from the ship after our visit. Her initial coolness towards us was understandable. She had been profiled in a 1971 *National Geographic* article ("Housewife at the End of the World,"[23] a chauvinistic title but National Geographic sponsored some of her scientific work). Bruce Chatwin had written about her also, unflatteringly, in his book, *In Patagonia*. Natalie may have been naturally reticent but she was obviously sick of "celebrity-seekers."

When Captain Lenie arrived, I explained why I particularly wanted to visit the *Hero*. "Ah, you're the one," he said. "I always wondered what happened to you after we lost radio contact."

He was a small, middle-aged man, about 5'3", with blue eyes and very red hair. He had a short waist and stood straight but walked with a forward tilt, like the wooden figures with moveable legs which scurry down if you put them on an incline. "Better you than me," he said when he found out Kathy and I were on bikes.

He added that our timing was good since they were leaving in a few days on an oceanographic research trip.

The *Hero* was tied up at a dock adjacent to several Argentine navy ships. She was a wooden-hulled, diesel-powered vessel, 125 feet long and shaped like a large trawler with two masts and a blunt bow, similar to an icebreaker. Commissioned to supply the U.S. Palmer base in Antarctica during the short Antarctic summers, she served as a research vessel at other times of the year. She had accommodations for six or more scientists, in addition to her regular crew of twelve. She looked as though she had weathered more than a few storms.

Captain Lenie had been eating dinner when Natalie called him. He took us to the ship's dining room and introduced us to Bruce, the chief engineer, whom Captain Lenie designated to show us around the vessel. Marco, the cook, asked if we'd like to eat dinner aboard first. Yes! We had roast beef, potatoes, creamed peas, and watermelon for dessert. Then Bruce gave us a tour of the ship. The *Hero* had been built in 1968 in Maine. Her wooden hull gave her extra resiliency and the rounded bow enabled her to ride up on ice floes, while more modern ships with sharper bows were more likely to get stuck. She was a solid, functional vessel but Bruce told us she was scheduled to be retired the next year because the U.S. Antarctic Research Program personnel wanted a ship like *Polar Stern*, a German vessel with fancy accommodations, a swimming pool, etc. Bruce said that the *Polar Stern*'s crew was forced to drain their swimming pool, however, due to the heavy seas in Drake Passage, between Cape Horn and Antarctica.

Above: Hero *at Palmer Station, Antarctica (Photo credit: National Oceanic and Atmospheric Administration Photo Library, Geodesy Collection)*

Bottom: Captain Pieter Lenie at dinner.

CHAPTER 3

Natalie came to the *Hero* to pick us up, as promised, and took us back to her house to retrieve our bikes. More talkative than she had been earlier, she asked questions about our trip and invited us, in an offhanded manner, to an *asado* (a sort of barbecue) to be held the following night as a send-off party for the *Hero's* crew.

Natalie introduced us to her husband, Tom Goodall. Born and bred on Tierra del Fuego, he was tall, lean and bearded. He spoke with a British accent and I asked him if he felt Argentine. "Oh, not at all," he replied, "I'm a British citizen." The Goodalls' two daughters, who were both away at college, were citizens of three countries: Britain, Argentina, and the U.S.

Tom said there was a joke among Argentines: Argentina should have declared war on the States, rather than Britain. The States would have flattened them, and Argentina would have come out of it like Japan and Germany.

Kathy asked, "Any hope for Argentina under Raúl Alfonsín?"[24]

"Lots of hope," Tom replied, "but it would take ten years of 'poverty.'" The Argentines would not be willing to put up with so much deprivation. The middle class was too comfortable.

Another joke: "When God made the world he said, 'I'm giving all the beautiful scenery to Argentina—the plants, the animals, the mineral riches.' Someone said, 'Hey, why are you giving it all to Argentina?' God said, 'Wait till you see the people I'm putting there.'"

This conversation took place in the corner of the Goodalls' basement where Tom was showing us his 1948 Raleigh bike with 28-inch wheels.

Thursday, February 9: Ushuaia is nestled in a spectacular setting, with an immediate backdrop of high, craggy mountains—the bottom of the Andes. Twelve miles to the west is Lapataia, the site of an old *estancia* and the southernmost terminus of the Pan American Highway (on which Kathy and

I had been riding, and which has as its northern terminus Prudhoe Bay, Alaska!). Lapataia sits on the Argentine-Chilean border and is the gateway to the spectacular Tierra del Fuego National Park.

The tourist bureau in Ushuaia recommended Lapataia as an excellent place for an afternoon excursion. Kathy and I shared a taxi with a tourist couple from Buenos Aires. My diary records that the woman had "diarrhea of the mouth," but our chauffeur-guide, Manuel Raúl Sapurón, was superb. He was a sensitive young man, locally born, who appreciated and loved his country and possessed an extensive knowledge of history, flora and fauna. His manners were beautiful; there was nothing false about him, just natural courtesy and consideration. He seemed to like the fact that we appreciated so much what he was showing us. Full of humility, he kept insisting that he was not a guide—a guide needed *"formación universitaria"*—four years at university. He said the university in Ushuaia specialized in engineering subjects, training local people for jobs in the oil and gas industries.

Manuel pointed out some of the most prevalent flora, including two different species of beech, wild raspberries that grew after forest fires, wild daisies, and a variety of mossy plants. He said that *turbales*—"boggy or marshy" areas in the valleys—were used for fertilizer. We got down on our knees to examine little red carnivorous plants called "mosquito catchers"— when a mosquito lands in the center of the tiny plant, the spines enclose the mosquito.

That evening we went to the *asado* at the Goodalls' house. Kathy and I took fixings for hot mulled wine, which was such a huge hit that we had to send out for more wine. Besides the crew of the *Hero*, the guests included an Argentine scientist and Captain Lenie's American wife, Betty, to whom we gave the leftover mulled wine mix. She invited us to come by the ship for coffee. I declined because Captain Lenie looked tired and probably had a great deal to do before the ship's departure the next day.

Kathy and I were the last guests to leave the *asado*. Natalie mentioned going to Harberton for the weekend to have some time to herself, but she was afraid she'd have to cook for a large group (15 people) scheduled to arrive at the *estancia* for sheep shearing. Harberton's regular cook would be spending the weekend in Ushuaia with her father, who was ill. Natalie asked Kathy and me, jokingly, if we could cook. Kathy said, "Réanne's fantastic in the kitchen!" Although I was keen to see Harberton, I wasn't sure about the catering and neither was Natalie. We all agreed to "think about it tonight and talk about it tomorrow."

Friday, February 10: In morning we went to see off the *Hero*. I gave Michael, the radio operator, a message for Don, since I was having trouble making international phone calls from Ushuaia. Michael gave me, in return, a message for his girlfriend in Punta Arenas and some patches for our jackets.

While we were at the dock we visited a French sailboat, *Spasiba,* which had a crew of two men, one in his thirties, the other much younger. They had left France three years earlier and planned to head from Ushuaia up the Patagonian canals, then to Puerto Montt, Valparaiso, etc. They expected to be in California within a year. I told them France had been my "second country" since the 1950s, when I spent a year in Grenoble as a college exchange student, and I returned there as often as I could. The two Frenchmen said we absolutely must "do" the French canals.

I tried again to call Don from the phone company (Entel) office, but the international lines were still down. "Everything to Río Grande cut."

In the afternoon we called again on Natalie to find out what she'd decided about the weekend. We said we would do it only if we could help and not be in the way. She was indecisive, then finally said "yes." We arranged to return to her house at 6 p.m. and called in at the tourist office to say that we were leaving Suarez' house in case someone else should want our room. Then we raced on our bikes to tell Heidi Suarez about our invitation and to collect our bags. Heidi was very excited for us and told us what she knew of Harberton. She didn't charge us for another night, even though it was 5 p.m. when we checked out.

Back to Natalie's. She was standoffish and said she had too many things to do to be ready to leave by 6 p.m. "Come back in an hour or so." We tried one more time at Entel. Same story—the lines were still down. Back once more to Natalie's. She said now that we would not be leaving until tomorrow morning, but Kathy and I could sleep at her house. She added that Don had called after getting my message from the *Hero*. I asked how this was possible, since the lines were "cut." Natalie said her phone went through Buenos Aires. She offered to let me use it call Don, so I did, and got through to him in ten minutes.

Natalie was still busy organizing for the weekend, so Kathy and I left to get some supper at a place Heidi had suggested. At 9:30 p.m. the wait-staff started an audiovisual program on Tierra del Fuego. At 10 p.m. Kathy and I were still waiting for someone to take our order. At 10:15 p.m., intermission, we were served orange soda. We decided to leave and found another restaurant five blocks away. "What's the quickest thing we can order?"

"Milanesa, five minutes."

We scarfed it down and went back to Natalie's. No problem. She was still up and doing things.

Saturday, February 11: My 51st birthday. When I woke, Kathy sang "Happy Birthday" to me and presented me with a little souvenir of Ushuaia—beech tree leaves under glass.

We left for Harberton in the late morning. During the drive, Natalie remained somewhat distant towards us. However, when Kathy mentioned that it was my birthday, Natalie said she would bake me a chocolate cake.

Estancia Harberton is on the Beagle Channel 50 miles east of Ushuaia. The first *estancia* on Tierra del Fuego, it was established by the pioneer missionary Thomas Bridges in 1886. The land was a gift from the Argentine government for Bridges' thirty years of work among the Yahgan Indians, for his assistance to numerous shipwrecked sailors, and for his role in the establishment of Ushuaia. It was named for his wife Mary's home village in Devon, England. Perhaps there was some geographical resemblance. In his book, *In Patagonia*, Bruce Chatwin said that in coming to Harberton from the land side, "you could mistake it for a big estate in the Scottish Highlands, with its sheep fences, sturdy gates and peat-brown trout streams."[25] I have never been to Scotland, but I don't doubt Chatwin's comparison. The *estancia* includes four large mountains, many lakes and swamps, and a stretch of coastline that includes several bays and a long narrow peninsula where the buildings are situated. Several islands in the Beagle Channel are also part of Harberton.

Kathy and I found the lawns and garden beautiful, but the *estancia's* buildings were in a state of disrepair. The main house, which had been imported in pieces from England and lived up to Chatwin's description of a "Victorian parsonage,"[26] was in dire need of a coat of paint, and there were loose steps and nails sticking up in places. Kathy and I felt Natalie was probably embarrassed by its condition, which might have been the reason for her hesitation in inviting us to join her and Tom over the weekend.

Natalie complained after our arrival that she was coming down with a cold, and she put herself to bed for a while after lunch, but she still insisted she would make the cake. She gave me her grandmother's recipe:

Top: Outbuildings, Estancia Harberton.

Bottom: Natalie and Tom Goodall.

3 eggs

2 cups sugar

3 cups flour (put in last)

or 2.5 cups flour and

½ cup oatmeal

powdered chocolate

2 cups milk

vinegar (or buttermilk)

baking powder

vanilla

salt

Frosting: can of condensed milk and bar of chocolate.

Tom Goodall was more outgoing than Natalie. He enjoyed talking with us about politics, the cultivation of vegetables in California, and his computer, and he delighted in showing us his terraced flower garden beyond the house. Natalie had asked one of us to pick flowers and arrange them, and the other to pick strawberries and raspberries. I picked a few flowers from the front and Tom came out and said, "Oh, there are more Canterbury bells up in the garden." He led me beside the house to a terraced garden bursting with lavender, Canterbury bells, pinks, lupine, pansies, forget-me-nots, honeysuckle, flowering sedum, snapdragons, and fuchsias.

The person we most enjoyed talking to at Harberton was Tom's mother, Clara Bridges de Goodall. She was 80 years old and full of memories of the *estancia* in its heyday as a farm. Listening to her made me very sentimental, thinking of my own mother with her marvelous descriptions of her life growing up. In 1920, Clara rode a horse from Río Grande to Harberton, declaring that it was a "wonderful time for young people to grow up among nature."

Clara had a rosy-complexioned face that was still beautiful and hands that looked no older than mine—large, farm-size hands with straight fingers. Although she had been out pitching hay the day before, she had given up horseback riding a year earlier because she was having attacks of

Clara Bridges de Goodall.

vertigo and was afraid she'd be a nuisance to the family if she fell off a horse. She talked about the Lucas Bridges Trail, which appeared on our map and ran north from Harberton to connect with the Ushuaia-to-Río Grande highway at the east end of Lago Fagnano. Clara said it had been a hiking and horse trail at one time—she used to ride it often—but the beavers had made a "mess of it." (She had warned Bruce Chatwin about the beavers when he set out to hike the Lucas Bridges Trail in 1975. He wrote of Clara packing him blackcurrant jam sandwiches and a thermos of coffee for the journey. The track had been rough and muddy, through forests and cattle pastures—and he had fallen into a beaver pond.)[27]

Kathy and I did not end up having to cook for the shearers, but we produced dinner for the Goodalls: salad and a huge lamb stew made from fresh tomatoes, carrots, potatoes, squash, green peas, spinach, parsley, 2 cups rosé and 1/2 cup of brandy. This was a great success with Tom Goodall and the house boy, Patricio, who both ate second helpings. For dessert, we had Hungarian crepes, plus Natalie's chocolate cake.

Kathy's diary: *Cooking in that kitchen was a real eye-opener. It was like going back a century. There was a huge wood cook-stove that kept the small room so hot I perspired profusely the whole time I was working. I thought of the phrase, "If you can't stand the heat, stay out of the kitchen," and understood that this was the kind of kitchen it referred to. Réanne and I had to "feed" the stove as we worked. There was no way to know what the temperature was on the black stovetop or in the oven. Réanne had cooked on a wood stove before and had a much better sense of it than I. As we prepared dinner, I was the sous-chef following her instructions. The meal was as good as she could have made at home—very good indeed!*

Sunday, February 12: Kathy and I washed dishes after breakfast, and I prepared a salad for the Goodalls' dinner while Kathy and Clara cracked crab.

After this, Kathy and I took a walk along the beach, looking for interesting rocks and bones. We found many bird bones and feathers from geese or cormorants, but no whale bones (though there were some of these in the Harberton garden). The rocks were coated in algae that ranged in color from bright goldenrod to almost orange and green. Just before lunch, I was overcome by an attack of nausea. Natalie served up a wonderful leg of mutton roasted in a wood oven, but I could eat only a very small piece of it, plus rice and raspberries. Afterwards I just had to go to bed. I resurfaced at 4 p.m. in time for tea, and then Kathy and I prepared to leave an hour later with a Goodall cousin, Martin, who would take us and our bikes to Rancho Hambre, on the main road north between Ushuaia and Garibaldi Pass. Martin and his wife arrived, and we put our bikes and bags in their pick-up truck. Clara and Patricio came out to say goodbye, and Clara said she hoped she would hear from us again. Natalie wished us well. She apologized for being sick and wrote an inscription in the front of my copy of her Tierra del Fuego guidebook:

> To Rianne,
>
> In memory of your visit to TF by bicycle – hoping that you have a safe and happy journey home and that you come back again.
>
> Con cariños,
> Natalie
> Harberton
> 12 Feb. 1984

CHAPTER 4

THE RETURN JOURNEY

I sat in the front of the pick-up going to Rancho Hambre, fighting nausea the whole time. Finally I couldn't overcome it and had to ask Martin to stop. I vomited up everything I'd eaten that day, so when Martin and his wife dropped us at Rancho Hambre, Kathy took charge. She pitched the tent, got out my sleeping bag, inflated my Thermarest, and fixed me some Tang. We camped about 300 yards from the government highway maintenance camp beside the river. It was 8 p.m. when I went to sleep.

Monday, February 13: After twelve hours' sleep I felt better but weak. Kathy and I packed up camp and tried to thumb a ride, but the few vehicles that passed didn't stop. We cycled to Paso Garibaldi, climbing up the south side and coasting down the north side. We rode 25 miles or so beyond the pass. The going was easy and pleasant because it was mostly downhill and gentle. Around 6 p.m., with Hostería Kaiken, at the far east end of Lago Fagnano, still two hours away and the wind in our faces, we were getting tired and decided to try thumbing. A pick-up with two men stopped. They said they were going to Kaiken; both worked at the Hostería. But it would be difficult for us to find rooms, they said, because of the excursion buses bringing tourist groups.

At the Hostería we met the manager, who was much more courteous than the young man we had dealt with on our southbound journey. I asked for a room, "*doble o simple.*" We would be happy to use our sleeping bags.

"*Va a ser muy difícil,*" because of the excursion buses.

We kept at it—"even a '*dormitorio arriba*'."

"Look, if you can wait until 8 or 8:30, I'll know, when the excursion bus comes in."

"If there's no room, could we camp nearby?"

"No problem, anywhere."

The manager showed us to the garage where we could leave our bikes and said that if there was anything we needed, just let him know. We had tea and sat around waiting and talking until 8:30 p.m. When the bus came in, "*Muy mala suerta.* (Very bad luck.)" So we went up the hill, pitched the tent by the path above the lake and went back to the Hostería for supper. The waiter was horrible, the service exceedingly slow, so at 11 p.m. we decided to forego dessert and went to bed.

I think the attack of vomiting Sunday was due to the fact that I'd been used to carbohydrates and exercise. Saturday night we had such rich stew and greasy *paliscinta*, then mutton again for Sunday dinner, that I think my intestines just closed down. Kathy said she and her husband had a similar experience after returning from a backpacking trip, and I recalled that Don had, too. Clearly, the mutton was just too fatty and rich for my stomach. Bruce Chatwin expressed a similar complaint in a letter to his wife: "It will take many years to recover from the roast lamb..."28

Tuesday, February 14: We caught a morning bus from Kaiken to Río Grande. The driver was very accommodating about our bikes, rearranging the back storage area to make room for them without our having to take the bikes apart.

We arrived in Río Grande by 10:45 a.m. Near the airport, we passed thousands of used oil drums, presumably leftover from the Falklands War.

The town showed signs of economic growth. Casio was building a new calculator factory near the airport; Telefunken was also constructing a new plant. The bus driver told us that the Argentine government gave tax breaks to businesses that came to Tierra del Fuego.

We stopped in Río Grande long enough to mail a package with a thank you note to the Goodalls, then headed out of town on our bikes. Reaching the outskirts, we started thumbing but no one stopped. Riding was impossible with the wind so strong, so we pushed and thumbed as we walked. A van stopped but the driver told us he was going only a few miles down the road, so Kathy said, "No, we'll wait for another one." I was extremely pissed and took off pushing and walking way ahead. Then I turned around suddenly and saw three pick-ups coming. I stuck out my thumb. One truck stopped. They were oilmen going near San Sebastián. They dropped us at the *Policia Internacional*, San Sebastián, on the Argentine side of the border. We cleared customs, international police, and passport control, and started cycling.

There were no trucks so we cycled the 10 miles to the Chilean San Sebastián, arriving just after 7 p.m. Not bad for cycling straight into headwinds! We cleared Chilean customs and would have liked to make Las Flores that night because the ground at the border was covered with clumps of "*coillon*," stiff, sharp grass which even sheep avoid. The thought of a night's sleep on top of that stuff would have kept us cycling under different circumstances, but we'd spent twelve hours battling 40-knot head winds, rain showers, and dust devils and were hungry and exhausted, our joints crying for rest. We decided to pitch camp near the police station, thinking we would just have a quick cup of soup and crawl into our sleeping bags.

I went to ask one of the policemen if camping there was okay, and if he had hot water, to save us the trouble of boiling our own. No problem to camp and, yes, he had hot water.

Welcome back to Chile!

CHAPTER 4

A few minutes later, we were unloading our gear when a voice asked in Spanish: "What are you doing?

We looked up simultaneously. A young *carabinero* astride a chestnut stallion smiled at us. He was dressed in an immaculate uniform and polished black riding boots; the antithesis of our dirty Plumline cycling outfits. Following him on another horse was a young civilian.

"We're getting ready to camp," Kathy replied.

"Oh, don't do that. I have room at my house. You can sleep there. There's hot running water for a shower, too."

"Oh really?" Kathy said. "Your family won't mind?"

"No problem. Just come to the yellow house over there," he said pointing, and the two of them trotted away.

"Dammit, Kathy, you were awfully quick to accept."

"Yeah, I surprised myself. The offer of a shower got me, I guess. We could tell him we prefer to camp."

"I suppose it's okay. A shower sounds awfully good to me, too!"

We wheeled our bikes across the road. The sky blackened and dumped on us as we dismantled our bags and walked up the front steps. The door was open, giving a glimpse of a living-room. Porcelain dinnerware, wine goblets, and demitasse cups gleamed behind the sliding glass doors of a highly polished buffet. Crocheted runners decorated the tops of the buffet and dining table. "Touches of the feminine," I thought.

"*Hola*," Kathy called, expecting to be greeted by the *carabinero's* wife. Instead, the young civilian greeted us. "My name is Mario,"* he said. "Please come in."

He led us down a hall, opened the door to a bedroom and told us to put our gear on the floor. "The bathroom's over here. You can shower

* Names have been changed.

87

when you like."

The "extra" bedroom was empty. No bed, no chair, no rug. Just a polished hardwood floor and a lace curtain at the window. "Well, it's *coillon* or this," I said. "And I guess we've committed ourselves." We unpacked our Thermarest mattresses and laid out our sleeping bags.

I went to take my shower while Kathy visited with Mario in the living room. The bathroom was as immaculate as the *carabinero's* uniform. Soap, cleanser, scrub brushes, deodorant, toothpaste, everything neatly placed. Too neatly. No ring in the tub, no hair gummed at the drain, no urine stains around the rim of the toilet. Curious, I opened the medicine cabinet. The same: everything in place.

"This guy's too tidy to be married," I thought. Besides, there was no lipstick, no eyeshadow, no mascara, no nail polish, no perfume, no hairspray, accoutrements that follow any self-respecting South American female. Obviously we'd hit upon bachelors.

I recalled an incident from thirty years earlier when, as a student in France, I'd let a friend talk me into taking a weekend tour to Yugoslavia with two Italian men. "We've got separate rooms, and they've promised to behave," she assured me. And of course they did. Like any Italian male would on a trip with two young women. We spent the entire Saturday night fighting them off, causing such a commotion in the hotel that at 3 a.m., the manager asked us all to leave.

"You were twenty then," I told myself. "What on earth makes you think there could be any similarity. These guys are probably just curious about two middle-aged *gringas*."

I hopped into the tub and turned on the shower. The water trickled out, as if from a tired hose. No matter; it was warm. I shampooed, lathered and stood under the trickle until my skin broiled. Pure luxury. I put on my one going-to-town outfit, a dirty turtleneck and damp, wrinkled jeans, dabbed some lipstick on my lips, and returned to the living-room.

"You look different," Kathy said.

"Yeah, I feel human now. Your turn."

She and Mario had just finished a checkers game. They'd polished off two glasses of Tang with brandy—our emergency health rations—and were discussing urban crime problems in the States. Mario was an officer with InterPol and had spent four weeks training in Washington, D.C. I noticed he'd switched to the informal Spanish "*tú*" when he talked to Kathy.

She glanced at me with a smile that translated as "Here we go..." and excused herself to take a shower.

Mario continued the discussion, questioning me about politics under the Reagan Administration, problems of American youth, U.S. opinion on the Falklands War. He was well informed and a good conversationalist, but I was irritated. It was nine o'clock and we hadn't eaten a real meal since morning.

"Look," I said, "suppose Kathy and I go ahead and prepare our dinner?"

"Oh no, don't do that. We'll prepare dinner when Roberto returns." No explanation about where he was or when he'd be back. I stewed.

Kathy rejoined us. Her blond, shoulder-length hair, braided since our last shower three days earlier, hung shining, full and sexy around her face. If the "before" interested Mario, he was sure to light up now.

Roberto finally appeared, perspiring and out of breath. He'd been jumping his horse, a nightly two-hour regimen. He smiled: "We'll prepare dinner after I shower."

Kathy and I fixed ourselves some instant soup and were getting ready to try a retreat to our sleeping bags when Roberto came into the kitchen carrying two bottles of wine. He was wearing a white polo shirt—Christian Dior—and tan Levis, and had slicked his black hair with oil. He reeked of shaving lotion.

"Now, a toast to our guests," he said, opening the wine and quoting a love poem of Pablo Neruda.

Ignoring the reference to love, I said, "Kathy is a poet."

"Ah? I write poetry also. Later I will show it to you."

I took a sip of the wine, excellent Chilean Cabernet. The guy had good taste.

"Now, Mario and I will prepare dinner for you: a leg of mutton from the ranch across the road, fresh tomatoes and lettuce from the garden. You and Katherine relax and listen to music."

Leg of mutton! I could see the program. Another three hours. It was 10 p.m. "I'm sorry, but we must go to bed early when we're cycling," my irritation obvious.

"Just thirty minutes. We will hurry. Mario can cook the mutton steaks and I will make the salad. Come," he said, pulling Kathy and me into the living room.

"Do you like typical Chilean music? I'll start with music of Tierra del Fuego."

Dinner was served at 10:45 p.m. Roberto kept up a commentary as he led us, musically, from the Ultimate South up the Chilean Coast. His appreciation of his own country impressed me. I'd never met an American Army officer who could talk about anything other than football, pop music, and beer.

We finished dinner at 11:45 p.m. Kathy rolled her eyes. I yawned. "That was delicious, but now we must go to bed." The two of us stood up, grabbed our dishes, and started toward the kitchen.

"Oh, don't bother, Mario and I will do the dishes in the morning. Besides, you haven't heard the music of the North yet," he said, jumping up to change the cassette.

Roberto and Mario sat on the sofa. Kathy and I took easy chairs facing them. "Are you single or married?" Mario asked.

"Married," I said quickly. Kathy had recently divorced but I hoped she wouldn't mention it. "Me too," she nodded.

"How do your husbands allow you to come on a trip like this?"

"They don't 'allow.' We're equals," Kathy said. "We just planned the trip and came." I did not go into the fact that Don had wanted to come with us, and that it had taken him several months to come to terms with my resolve to "uninvite" him. "Equal" was not as straightforward as it sounded.

Music of the North clicked off. "Just a little romantic music for dancing," Roberto said as he jumped up to change cassettes.

"Oh damn," I thought, "here comes the test."

"No!" Kathy said abruptly. "We're too tired for dancing. Besides, we're old enough to be your mothers."

They both laughed. "How old do you think we are?"

"About twenty-five," I said.

"On no, we're both thirty-two and you can't be more than thirty-five."

"Oh yes we are," Kathy said raising her voice. "She's even a grandmother," pointing at me.

Stunned, they slumped back on the sofa. "You're lying," Roberto said.

I shook my head.

"How old are you?"

Conditioned by our youth-worshipping culture in the States where forty was okay but fifty was the downhill run, I didn't want to admit I'd just begun the run. I knew Kathy wasn't about to reveal her age; she was always reminding me that she's the younger by three and a half years.

"We're over forty," I said.

"Impossible! How do you stay in such good shape? South American grandmothers don't look like you."

"We can look at the Customs records tomorrow if you won't tell us your ages," Mario said.

"Fine," I thought. By the time they knew our ages we'd be a dozen miles down the road and the joke would be on them. I could see the other officers laughing. "Tried to pick up some grannies, did you?"

"I'm going to bed," Kathy said heading down the hall. "Come on, Réanne."

"Just one dance, please," Roberto begged, wrapping his arms around my shoulders. "Does the difference in our ages bother you?"

"Of course."

"It doesn't bother me."

"Look, we wouldn't have stayed if we'd thought you were confused about our ages." I struggled not to giggle—this had all the elements of a Spanish melodrama. But I'd be asking for trouble if I laughed at him. Latin machismo is notorious.

"Réanne! Help!" Kathy's voice was guttural.

"Good night, Roberto." I pushed his arms away. "I'm just not interested."

I ran down the hall. Mario had Kathy pinned to the wall.

"What the hell were you doing! I need help. This guy's drunk!"

"Come on, Kathy," I said in Spanish, prying Mario from her and shoving him onto the floor. "Time for bed."

We shut the door. There was no way to lock it. No bolt or key. Not even a chair to jam against it. I switched off the light. We slid into our bags, jeans and shirts still on.

The door opened. "You okay?" Mario shouted. He turned on the light. We lay still, pretending to be asleep. He slammed the door, re-opened it, turned the light on again, slammed the door a second time.

"God, they must be hard up," Kathy said. "Just us and the sheep."

The door opened a third time and we heard Roberto say, "Leave them alone, Mario."

"If I ever come back to South America," Kathy said, "I'll dye my hair dull gray and wrap it in a granny bun."

Kathy's reflections on this episode: *"Gawd, how could I have been so stupid," I thought to myself as I lay in the dark, my heart pounding against my ribs, hoping the door wouldn't open again and that I could get to sleep. I was exhausted, scared, and uncomfortable on the hard wood floor. But Réanne and I had been riding and hitching alternately for three days, in wind and rain, and camping out. I had felt gritty and I knew I smelled. My clothes smelled even worse than I did, and they were not what anyone would have considered "sexy." And I was 47. My days as a sex symbol were over. I'd begun to feel invisible in lines at the grocery store, at the bank, and in other public places. The world was full of younger, more vibrant women. Why would twenty-something Chilean men even look at me? Ditto with Réanne. So it simply didn't occur to either of us that a policeman offering a couple of grungy travelers a place to sleep would be anything more than a gesture of kindness on his part. How were we to know that he would be living alone out here, and that he and his friend probably hadn't seen anything more attractive than a young ewe for God knows how long? And "Mario" seemed genuinely interested in American politics and culture. I finally got it only when the lieutenant joined us after his shower wearing enough cologne to scent a whole battalion. Réanne and I exchanged looks: Oh boy, how do we get out of this one?*

Wednesday, February 15: Our alarm clock rang at 6 a.m. We had slept poorly. Hard floor, stuffy room. *Coillon* and fresh air forsaken for love of a shower. "Let's get the hell out of here," I said. We used the bathroom before Roberto got up, packed our bags and carried our stuff out front. I went back to check that we hadn't left anything. Roberto was up and dressed by then. He looked a bit sheepish, said goodbye, and embraced me in the Chilean way. There was no sign of Mario.

Kathy and I waited for the bus. When it came, the driver said, "*Llenado.* (Full.)" Couldn't take us. Another bus would arrive in a couple of hours, but I was keen to put San Sebastián behind us. "Let's get out of here and see if we can hitch," I said. "We'll try to get to La Nonna's."

The wind was in our faces as usual. On the edge of San Sebastián, I saw a parked truck with a Porvenir license plate. I stopped and asked the driver if he was going to Porvenir. "*A las 7 de la tarde,*" he said. "At 7 p.m."

I hollered, "If you see us on the route this evening, can you take us to Porvenir?" He said, "sure."

At the junction of the "highway" to Porvenir with the road to Bahía Azul, to the north, we passed a guy standing by the big road sign. He had a big clipboard in his arms. I thought he was waiting for the bus. Turned out he was counting the vehicles. He fitted right into Bruce Chatwin's "archetypical" Tierra del Fuegian scene of "crossroads of insignificant importance with roads leading in all directions, apparently to nowhere."[29]

No one came by with whom we could hitch a ride, so we cycled the seven miles to Las Flores. It took us nearly two hours, straight into the wind the entire way. I drafted behind Kathy when I could, but most of the time I just plugged along a few hundred yards behind her.

We were both steamrollered by the time we reached Las Flores. It was mid-morning by then and La Nonna made us tea and toast and insisted we stay for lunch. She asked where we had slept, saying that we could have stayed at her house. "We tried, but were too tired." This part was true, but we did not want to tell her we had slept in the *carabinero's* house. I lied and said we camped outside but had dined with the lieutenant.

"Fine person," she said.

Later she asked why we hadn't stayed inside his house. Kathy said,

"Because we didn't want to." La Nonna said she understood and laughed her deep laugh.

Just before noon the man who'd been counting cars at the Porvenir-to-Bahía Azul intersection arrived at La Nonna's for lunch. Again, he said he would take us in his truck to Porvenir at 7 p.m. So Kathy and I decided to spend the afternoon at La Nonna's, resting and writing in our journals until he returned. After lunch of mutton soup, pasta with mutton (which, as in Harberton, did not agree with me), Kathy and I laid our sleeping bags out on the lawn and slept outside for three hours. The sun was shining and the afternoon was beautiful and quite warm. I could have slept on, but we got up around five and had tea, fresh bread and butter with "*ribarbo*" jam.

The truck arrived at 6:30 p.m.; we loaded up, said goodbye to La Nonna, and left.

By the time we arrived in Porvenir it was 9:45 p.m.—too dark to cycle on to Bahía Chilota. We rode to the center of town, looking for a hotel. The young man who had helped us find the Hostería on our first night in town happened to be walking down the street with two other friends and saw us. Kathy recognized him right away. He asked how our trip had gone and did we want to go to the same hotel? No, we hoped to find a closer one. He pointed to the Hotel Central, on the corner of the next block. "Clean rooms. *Baño, casi privado*, nice." We were the only guests.

Thursday, February 16: My diary records that the "sun rose at 6:56 above the top of the hills at the southeast end of Bahía Porvenir."

The hotel proprietor was a short, attractive young woman. She wore a wedding ring but we saw no sign of a husband. She had frosted hair and teeth filled with white porcelain which didn't match the color of her natural teeth so, at first glance, she appeared to be wearing braces. She told us she was born in Porvenir and she had studied in Valdivia, on the southern

Chilean mainland, but she had come back because of "*falta de trabajo* (lack of work)." She said this with a wistful twist of her mouth.

Kathy and I cycled to Bahía Chilota after breakfast. I hoped we would catch up with my teacher-friend Eli Ruiz. Her family lived in Bahía Chilota, near the ferry dock, but we had not managed to see them when we passed through earlier.

Eli's parents, Señor and Señora Ruiz and their younger daughter, Flora, were at home, but Eli was in Punta Arenas. Couldn't we stay the night, they asked, and have a *curanto* (a traditional Chilean barbecue) the next day when Eli came back on the *barcaza* for the weekend? They would kill a *lechon* (suckling pig) for us. No, we couldn't, we had to catch the *barcaza* at 1 p.m. that day. If we were to see Eli, it would have to be in Punta Arenas.

Though the surrounding landscape is dry and flat, Bahía Chilota is picturesque, with piles of shells along the shore, fishing boats lying about, and lots of ducks and geese. Kathy and I took pictures on the beach along the entrance to the bay under gray sky, using up all but one frame of our last roll of film. We looked for interesting shells or bones. Kathy found a lamb's head with small horns, one slightly longer than the other; many sea urchin shells; and other hat-like shells. Nothing as interesting as whale bones, however, although Kathy was quite entranced by a vintage diver's helmet we found on the beach. She desperately wanted to take it home, but we couldn't figure out any way to do it.

We returned to the Ruiz house for an early lunch: delicious fresh *centolla* (spider crab) for the first course with homemade *mayonesa*; for the main course, lettuce-and-tomato salad with fresh boiled potatoes (all produce from the garden) and fresh *robalo* (a local fish). While we were eating, the *barcaza* came in, dropped off its passengers and went to the *muelle* (pier) in town, supposedly to fill up on water. At 1 p.m., the time it was due to leave, the ferry still had not returned. At 2 p.m., no *barcaza*; nor at 2:30 p.m. We started to worry a little. We had called Rina in the morning to tell her we'd be in Punta Arenas about 4 p.m. We were not the only people waiting. Every hour someone said, "The *barcaza* is leaving at X hour," 'X' being 4 p.m., 6 p.m., 11 p.m., etc.

To pass the time we talked to a woman from Punta Arenas, who was waiting in a pick-up truck with her husband. She had a nice sense of humor and understood our frustration. The Ruizes wanted us to stay all night. Flora kept talking about what they would cook if we stayed until Saturday. Kathy was more frustrated than I, trying to write her diary with kids hanging around asking constant questions. Finally, I suggested we clean our bikes and bags.

I liked Señor Ruiz, Eli's father, very much. He was short and swarthy, with a cryptic sense of humor. Example: The population of Porvenir at that time was 7,000. Kathy and I couldn't figure out why so many people would live there.

Flora Ruiz, trying on my bicycle for size.

"*Militares. Todos militares,*" Señor Ruiz said.

"*Que hacen?* (What do they do?)," I asked.

"*Comen y duermen* (They eat and sleep)," he replied.

We finished cleaning our bikes, took another walk, and heard that the ferry would leave at 6 a.m. the next morning. Kathy and I decided to camp, but the Ruizes wouldn't hear of it.

"I have to get up early," Señor Ruiz said. "I'll keep an eye on the *barcaza* and wake you when it's time."

Kathy's recollection: *The Ruizes were among the kindest and most hospitable people I have ever met. They were genuine, and even though they were poor they would have shared their last clam with us. The night we spent in their house is one I—and my back—will always remember. The bed Réanne and I slept on was barely twin-sized with a thin mattress, but the most troublesome feature was that it was approximately U-shaped—it went up at the ends and had a crater at the center. One person could have slept rolled up in a ball or kind of cattywampus and maybe found a reasonably comfortable position, but with two of us neither could turn without upheaving the other. I couldn't sleep on my back comfortably for long because of an injury, and sleeping on my side was impossible because of the curvature of the bed, so I squirmed, turned when I could no longer bear not to, and longed for the comfort of the floor I had slept on the night before, in the lieutenant's house at the border.*

Friday, February 17: 6 a.m. came and went. Still no *barcaza*—but Kathy and I were tired of waiting. We would miss Eli, but we *had* to get to Punta Arenas that day.

We loaded our bikes and rode back into Porvenir, thinking we might have to take an airplane to Punta Arenas. On our way to town we visited the *barcaza* at the pier to ask if we could leave our bikes and pick them up when they eventually made it to Punta Arenas. Captain Raúl said he would take care of them personally.

Kathy went to one airline agency, I went to another. Tama Airlines had a flight leaving at 12:45 p.m., so I booked and paid for two seats, 600 pesos each (US$6.85). Kathy had made reservations for the first open flight on the other airline, leaving 8 p.m. that night.

We left our bags at Tama Airline, rode our bikes to the *barcaza*, and left them on board. Captain Raúl said it looked like the *barcaza* would leave at 1 p.m.

We traveled in a "micro" (bus) to the airport, which was busier than Porvenir itself. The plane, a 10-seater Cessna, left on time. Dark clouds were piling up from the east. The pilot kept looking eastward with a worried look in his face. Me, too. I thought of the French writer and aviator Antoine de Saint-Exupery, who had flown in Patagonia as a mail pilot in the late 1920s. He wrote that the winds were so strong they made his plane fly "backward."[30] Fortunately, our own aircraft continued to fly "forward" and landed in Punta Arenas just before the rain hit.

Rina and Sergio met us at the airport in Punta Arenas. As we picked up our bags to take them to their car, I saw Roberto—the Don Juan from San Sebastián—walking out of the terminal. I said, "Oh shit, Kathy, the *carabinero*—Roberto—is just coming out!"

Kathy and I both looked the other way. Roberto climbed aboard the airport "micro" bus. Kathy and I got in the car with Sergio and Rina and drove to their house.

Map 5: Punta Arenas to Puerto Montt & Isla de Chiloé

Buenos Aires •

Puerto Montt

Isla de Chiloé

ARGENTINA

CHILE

SOUTH ATLANTIC OCEAN

SOUTH AMERICA

Falkland Islands

Puerto Edén

• Torres del Paine

Puerto Natales

Strait of Magellan

Punta Arenas

SOUTH PACIFIC OCEAN

Tierra del Fuego

Ushuaia

Puerto Williams

Cape Horn

0   150   300 kilometers

0   100   200   300 miles

CHAPTER 5

BEYOND TIERRA DEL FUEGO

We spent the next two days with Rina and Sergio and several other friends in Punta Arenas. They were one of the major reasons I had wanted to return to that part of the world. I felt bad that I wasn't able to see as much of them as I hoped because of the ferry delay and other complications—but I was still glad to have done the bike trip. In 1975, my teacher-friend Pepa's husband Humberto had invited Don and me to make use of his ham radio during our enforced stay in Punta Arenas. Humberto had died of cancer in December 1983, and Pepa's daughter had been ill also. Our reunion with Pepa was an emotional one, and she and her son, Gonzalo, both came to the bus station to say goodbye when Kathy and I left for Puerto Natales on February 21. Rina, Sergio and Mauricio waved us off also.

Pepa and Gonzalo.

Rina Gacitua de Araneda.

Torres del Paine.

Although Kathy and I rode a bus from Punta Arenas to Puerto Natales, our bikes had to come separately by truck the following day. In Puerto Natales, we stayed in an extremely squalid hotel but took a day to visit Torres del Paine National Park. Seventy miles north of Puerto Natales, this is an unspoiled region of absolutely stunning scenery—mountains, glaciers, lakes and waterfalls—dominated by the distinctive, 9,000-foot granite spires of the Cordillera del Paine. Kathy and I took a small tour van to get there, then hiked around the shores of Lago Grey and onto the icy slopes. On the way we saw a magnificent waterfall and herds of wild guanacos—the llama-like herbivores of Patagonia.

The following day, we boarded a boat, *Las Evangelistas*, for a 3-day cruise up the Patagonian canals to Puerto Montt. *Las Evangelistas* was a coastal supply ship, as basic as they come, with a few cramped, airless, "cattle class" cabins available for tourists. Some passengers slept on blankets on the floor of the lounge. Kathy and I slept on extremely narrow berths in a two-person cabin.

Several of our fellow tourists were motorcyclists who had been riding around Patagonia but vowed "never again." They had flat tires every day,

Las Evangelistas.

and sometimes more than one a day. They were amazed when Kathy and I told them we hadn't had any flats on our bicycle trip.

Entry from my diary, February 23: *On a ship like this all I do is sit from a throne looking down on more of the same: mountains, sometimes forested, sometimes glacier-polished without vegetation, admiring the waterfalls and streams which tumble down into the* canales *but I don't feel a part of it. Everything looks alike from here. More of the same every nautical mile: mountains, streams, islands, valleys, waterfalls, streams, fog, rain, snow unrelated to my senses after I've seen 10 miles of it. On Le Dauphin Amical each mile brought a new discovery—a new cove that offered protection or terror. From the bridge of* Las Evangelistas *I can't even see the coves or anchorages. Even the ship's charts are such small-scale that the anchorages aren't named. Puerto Mayne so far is the only one that has been named on charts.*

At 11 a.m. we anchored at Puerto Eden. As we arrived about 30 wooden boats set off from shore to meet our boat. Whole families came with bags of fresh mussels, crabs, and smoked mussels strung on grass to be sold and traded for sheep, flour, etc. A civil engineer from Valparaiso traveling with his 11-year-old son explained to me that the people at Puerto Eden are seldom without contact for more than a week at a time because of the boat traffic. Several people got off at Eden.

Women with handmade souvenirs—baskets and miniature canoes—came on board to sell their wares: miniature canoe 50 pesos each, baskets 100 pesos each. Sheep were lowered by rope to the wooden boats or carried on the shoulders of the men. At 11:30 a.m. the horn blew for everyone to board and for the Edenses to get off. The boats cast off with bags of flour, live sheep, lamb carcasses and whatever remained unsold.

Later that same day the ship approached San Pedro Point, an island with a lighthouse, and slowed to a stop. Although it was not yet dark, visibility was almost nil due to pouring rain mixed with hail and sleet. Rumors among the half-dozen English-speakers on board were: 1) we were going to anchor and wait for better weather; 2) the crew needed to repair something; 3) they

Above and below: Exchange of goods in Puerto Eden.

were taking all the first class passengers ashore for an *asado*; 4) they were taking some people ashore to do some research. The latter turned out to be true—three meteorologists were going ashore to study the weather conditions for three months. What was there to learn, we wondered. . . That the weather is always *malo, malo?*

After dark, we entered the exposed waters of Golfo de Penas. *Las Evangalistas* rolled, slammed, cracked for most of the night. At times the pounding was so bad I would awaken with the blasphemous thought, "Jesus Christ, I hope this boat holds together." Many of the passengers were sick. Kathy showed up for all of the meals, but I stayed in my berth until we re-entered calmer waters. Not that I was seasick particularly, but the food on board ship was the worst we'd had in South America in five weeks—tripe and fish mush. Visibility was nil, in any case. There seemed little to get up for. Kathy and I tried to do some writing—our journals and notes on our bike trip—but the only places aboard ship we could do this were on the bridge and in the lounge. The noise in the lounge was deafening—guys playing *fusbol*, and a television showing a constant stream of C-grade American movies.

Kathy: *On the map the archipelago stretching north along the Chilean coast looks like it would be fascinating. I pictured deep fiords like those in Norway, so I was mightily disappointed that it was mostly solid, monotonous beech forest for almost the entire trip from Puerto Natales to Puerto Montt. We hadn't expected a luxury cruise, but were disappointed with the food, the boat and the scenery. Not something I would recommend or do again. But there was one memorable incident. In the lounge, movies played on the TV several times a day. Most of them weren't worth watching, but one afternoon the offering was "Tootsie," with Dustin Hoffman as an unemployed actor who dresses as a woman to get a job. I had seen it but Réanne had not and I talked her into watching it. I thought it a brilliant comedy and social commentary and well worth watching a second time. Most of the other passengers on the boat were laborers of various types, coming or going to their jobs. Few would have had more than a high school education. They were not a sophisticated crowd. "Tootsie" was in English with Spanish subtitles. As the story progressed, there were chuckles and a few points at which the audience really laughed, but mostly they sat with expressions of confusion and incredulity on their faces. The subtitles didn't begin to capture the complexity or nuance of the dialogue. I could not help wondering what these unworldly Latin males made of this film, with its mixed sexual messages and ambiguities. A lot was lost in translation.*

On February 25, at 9:15 p.m. we arrived in Puerto Montt. The ship had been running on one engine for most of the day. Everyone wondered why we were moving so slowly, but the reason was that we had to wait for high tide to dock. Then there were problems with the gangplank and it seemed we would all be spending another night aboard. Kathy and I had hoped we might at least be able to leave our bikes on the boat and retrieve them in the morning. But no, if we left, all our stuff had to go with us. Kathy and Bruce, a fellow American, went off to find a hotel. I stayed with the bikes. A young man wearing a poncho came over and started asking questions about where we came from, what we had done, where we were going, etc. He thought it was fantastic that we had cycled across Tierra del Fuego. I asked if he had come to meet the boat. He replied that he was a tourist who lived in Santiago. He had come down to the pier from his hotel to see *Las Evangelistas.* He said Kathy and I were the most interesting things to come off her by far. When I told him we were from California, he roared and said, "I knew it. You had to be from California. That's where everything starts. It begins there and runs around the world. *(Hay de todo en California. Empieza en California y se corre el mundo.)*"

From Puerto Montt we rode a bus and a ferry to Isla de Chiloé to visit Alfonso Bahamonde, the young Chilean fisherman who had crewed for

Don and me aboard *Le Dauphin Amical* in 1975. Alfonso and two South African backpackers, Margie and Trevor, sailed with us from Punta Arenas to Buenos Aires, where we undertook major repairs to the boat. I flew home from Buenos Aires to resume my teaching job in California, but Alfonso, Margie and Trevor stayed with Don and *Le Dauphin* and sailed together across the South Atlantic to Cape Town, then north to California via the Panama Canal. Don and I grew very fond of all three of our crew members, and I could not have left Southern Chile without seeing Alfonso.

He met us off the Isla Chiloé bus in his home town of Castro. He was in his mid-thirties by then but looked little different from when I had last seen him in 1975. I remembered him as an unworldly but cheerful young man, as well as an excellent cook! Now he owned a small fishing boat, the *Kon Tiki*, that he had bought with the money he had saved from his year as a crewman aboard *Le Dauphin*. He took us to the house of his sister and her family, where we stayed for the next two nights. They invited us to a party in an apple orchard at which an antique wooden press was used to make cider—an annual event in which everyone in the village participated. Alfonso also took us for a ride aboard *Kon Tiki*.

With Alfonso aboard his fishing boat, Kon Tiki.

Alfonso Bahamonde.

After several days on Isla de Chiloé, Kathy and I returned to Puerto Montt. From there we caught a flight to Santiago and another to Los Angeles, arriving there March 3. Don met us at the airport and was full of questions that we were too tired to answer immediately.

Don later wrote an amusingly colorful press release about our adventure: "Mud clogs bike, stove and tent—food runs low—women helped by friendly gauchos—Chilean and Argentine border guards overcome by such machismo!" He added that "age and sex need be no limit to personal accomplishment." Kathy and I had proved this to be true, at least to ourselves, though Don also assumed that, being women, "we cried a lot." In fact, neither Kathy nor I cried at all, at least during the cycling part of our trip. (We did, however, shed a few tears upon leaving our friends in Punta Arenas). Kathy's only concession to femininity was to pack her hair dryer; mine was to take lipstick.

Kathy wrote afterwards that the days of cycling, like her training, had been grim, but she could look back on them with both satisfaction and humor. Her pre-trip preparations had strengthened and hardened her body, and because she already knew from backpacking and sailing that discomfort was "seldom fatal," she could ignore the mental dictates of her trainer and others who said she couldn't do it. She also argued that age contributed its own strengths: "When we got to Ushuaia, Réanne and I both knew we had pedaled down a road neither of us would have had the courage to begin, nor the grit to finish at age twenty."[31]

As for me, what had I learned about myself? Don's and my sailing nightmare nine years earlier had taught me that the will to survive is the strongest instinct I have—that when my life depended on it, I could push myself far beyond what I had ever believed possible. But I had no desire to keep testing the limits, as Don did, just for the adventure of it. Life is too fragile. The cycling trip had taught me that I could choose my own challenges and derive deep satisfaction out of pushing myself within my own self-defined limits. I had proved that—on land where I was much more at home than at sea—I could take care of myself. And in doing this, I had exorcised the lingering demons of my first visit to Tierra del Fuego. The weather was every bit as bad as I remembered it, but I had gone back to confront it head-on—literally, for most of the 300 miles we had ridden! Yes, the going had been hard, with too few gears on roads that gave us at least as much grief as the wind, but Kathy and I had gripped the handle bars of our bicycles and pushed on.

EPILOGUE

A number of people asked me after our cycling trip if I would do it again. My unhesitating answer was "yes!" though in the intervening thirty years neither Kathy nor I have had the opportunity to repeat the experience. But I have been back to Tierra del Fuego twice, on non-cycling trips with my husband Don.

Don's long-held goal of sailing around Cape Horn had been aborted by our pitchpole experience in 1975, but he never gave up on the dream. In 1997, as a Christmas present, I bought him a berth on a sailboat called the *Mahina Tiare*, owned by an American-Kiwi couple, John and Amanda Neal, who have a business taking people on sailing expeditions. Don joined the boat in Puerto Williams, on the Chilean side of the Beagle Channel, and "rounded the Horn" from there during a three-week voyage. I accompanied Don as far as Puerto Williams but did not join the group. One voyage aboard a small boat in those latitudes was enough for me! But I was delighted to return to Tierra del Fuego, and I spent several days hiking in the hills above Puerto Williams before flying to Punta Arenas to visit our friends.

In 2008, I returned to Tierra del Fuego yet again, with Don, to board a small French cruise ship, *Le Diamant*, on a visit to Antarctica. We spent four days in Ushuaia before our voyage, and did a day trip to Harberton where we met with Natalie and Tom Goodall. They had spruced up the house and outbuildings and were running the *estancia* as a tourist destination. They had added a new tea room, as well as replica Yahgan huts, a restaurant, and a natural history museum. Regular bus tours ran from Ushuaia and the road to Harberton had been paved part way.[32]

After our Antarctic cruise, we flew home via Punta Arenas and Isla de Chiloé, where we enjoyed another visit with Alfonso Bahamonde.

Early in the crossing to Antarctica, I had presented a slide-show on Don's and my 1975 adventures aboard *Le Dauphin Amical. Le Diamant's* itinerary did not include a stop at Cape Horn. But on the return voyage the captain sought special permission from the Chilean authorities—and weather conditions on the day were such that Don and I and most of *Le Diamant's* other passengers were able to go ashore on Cape Horn Island. Don and I toured the lighthouse with the group, and the two of us were given exclusive permission to visit the compound of the Chilean officials who were stationed on the island. So, regardless of its fearsome reputation, Don and I both have extremely warm memories of "the uttermost part of the earth."

I have also revisited Tierra del Fuego numerous times vicariously, as Don and I spent nearly two decades cruising the Inside Passage of northern British Columbia and Alaska on our trawler, *Baidarka*, researching and writing a series of guidebooks for boaters. I realized during our 1997 return visit to southern Chile that the mountains and channels, waterfalls and glaciers, the forested islands, the wind and rain of the Pacific Northwest and Alaska are remarkably similar to the wild beauty that I fell in love with in the Canales de Patagonia. I can only conclude that these high-latitude landscapes are in my blood—but as I wrote in a 1998 magazine article,[33] I was happy by that stage of my life to continue my cruising in Alaska, but for my southern sightseeing I would rather fly to Punta Arenas and rent a four-wheel drive.

ENDNOTES

1 This phrase, often used as a description of Tierra del Fuego, comes from a 1949 memoir by the Fuegian-born writer and *estanciero* Lucas Bridges: *The Uttermost Part of the Earth* (New York: E.P. Dutton and Company, 1949).

2 The current (2015) population of Punta Arenas is around 123,000.

3 Goodall, Rae Natalie Prosser, *Tierra del Fuego*, 3rd edition (Buenos Aires: Ediciones Shanamaiim, 1978), p.32

4 I flew home from Buenos Aires to resume my teaching job. Don completed repairs to the boat in B.A., after which he sailed with Alfonso and two young South Africans across the Atlantic to Cape Town, then home to Los Angeles via the Panama Canal.

5 Goodall, *Tierra del Fuego*, p.20

6 Chatwin, Bruce, *In Patagonia* (New York: Penguin, 1977)

7 Goodall, *Tierra del Fuego*, p.21

8 Moorehead, Alan, *Darwin and the Beagle* (New York: Harper & Row, 1969), p.100

9 Goodall, *Tierra del Fuego*, p.21

10 Goodall, *Tierra del Fuego*, p.120

11 Dienes, Katherine, "Better Hard-Ass Than Expert – A woman listens to her body," *Bicycle Rider*, Summer 1985, p.59

12 Dienes, "Better Hard-Ass Than Expert," p.60

[13] Hemingway-Douglass, Réanne, *Cape Horn—One Man's Dream, One Woman's Nightmare* (Anacortes, Washington: Cave Art Press, 1994, 2003)

[14] Chatwin, *In Patagonia*, p.42

[15] Bridges, *The Uttermost Part of the Earth*, p.441

[16] Possibly a Fuegian fox (*Dusicyon culpaeus lycoides*)

[17] Hemingway-Douglass, Réanne and Katherine Dienes, "Against the Wind—Women and Bikes in the Land of Fire," *Cyclist*, October 1984, p.50

[18] Hemingway-Douglass and Dienes, "Against the Wind," p.50

[19] Winchester, Simon, *Outposts – Journeys to the Surviving Relics of the British Empire* (New York: Harper Perennial, 2003), p.279

[20] Goodall, *Tierra del Fuego*, 251. Of the tourists who visited in 1976-77, an estimated 40,000 arrived by plane, 8,000 by road (via Punta Arenas or the First Narrows, at the northern tip of Isla Grande), and 9,000 by ship. In the 2014-15 summer season the number of cruise ship passengers visiting Ushuaia was expected to top 100,000.

[21] Hemingway-Douglass and Dienes, "Against the Wind," p.52

[22] Saavedra, Julio C., *Southern Patagonia & Tierra del Fuego*, (Santiago: Turismo & Communicaciones S.A., 1994), p.47

[23] Goodall, Rae Natalie P., "Housewife at the End of the World," *National Geographic*, Vol. 139 (1), January 1971, pp.130-150

[24] Raúl Alfonsín, Argentina's first democratically elected president since the military junta of 1976-1983.

[25] Chatwin, *In Patagonia*, p.134

[26] Chatwin, *In Patagonia*, p.134

[27] Chatwin, *In Patagonia*, pp.139-141

[28] Shakespeare, Nicholas, *Bruce Chatwin—A Biography.* (New York: Nan A. Talese/Doubleday, 1999), p.3

[29] Shakespeare, *Bruce Chatwin*, p.313

[30] Saint-Exupery, Antoine, *Night Flight* (New York: Houghton Mifflin Harcourt, 1931, 1974)

[31] Dienes, "Better Hard Ass than Expert,"p. 61

[32] I was saddened to learn during the writing of this book that Natalie Goodall died in May 2015 at the age of 80.

[33] Hemingway-Douglass, Réanne, "Dreaming of Cape Horn," *Pacific Yachting*, March 1998

Photo credit, p. 66: Michelle Maria, Pixabay.com. CCO Public Domain.

ABOUT RÉANNE

Réanne Hemingway-Douglass grew up in the Great Lakes region and Washington D.C. She attended Pomona College, Claremont Graduate University in Southern California, and the Université de Grenoble, France. After teaching French for twenty years, she joined her husband, Don Douglass, in their manufacturing and backpacking business. In the 1970s she and Don were the first American couple to attempt a circumnavigation of the Southern Hemisphere by sailboat. Réanne's best-selling book, *Cape Horn: One Man's Dream, One Woman's Nightmare,* tells the story of their pitchpoling near Cape Horn. In her fifties, Réanne and her friend Katherine Wells were the first women to bicycle across Tierra del Fuego. Réanne's articles on bicycling, cruising and women's issues have appeared in numerous outdoor magazines. She and Don are the authors of a series of six detailed nautical guidebooks and maps from Baja Mexico to Prince William Sound, Alaska. Réanne is also the author of *The Shelburne Escape Line—Secret Rescues of Allied Aviators by the French Underground, The British Royal Navy and London's MI-9.* The Douglasses live on Fidalgo Island in Washington State, U.S.A.

ABOUT KATHERINE

Katherine Wells is a writer and artist. Born in Kansas City, she attended the University of Wyoming, after which she spent a year in Venezuela as a Fulbright scholar. She taught high school in Southern California for eleven years, then co-owned a graphic design/silkscreen business for the next decade. Following that she began a successful career as a mixed-media artist with twenty solo exhibitions to her credit. In 1992, Katherine moved to New Mexico and purchased a 188-acre parcel of land north of Santa Fe. She has since discovered nearly 10,000 petroglyphs on her property and has dedicated the last twenty years to their preservation. In 1999, she, her neighbors, and local archaeologists founded the Mesa Prieta Petroglyph Project. Katherine has been responsible for much of the fundraising and programming for the Project, and has guided it in nearly every aspect of its development, from its small origins to its present status as a highly respected 501(c)(3) organization with nearly 100 volunteers, one full-time staff archaeologist and two half-time employees. (For further information go to http://mesaprietapetroglyphs.org.) Katherine's 2009 memoir, *Life on the Rocks: One Woman's Adventures in Petroglyph Preservation* was published by the University of New Mexico Press. Her writing has also appeared in many poetry journals and magazines.